STANDARD GRADE
MODERN STUDIES
REVISION GUIDE

⊘ get **results**
Second Edition

Standard Grade Modern Studies Revision Guide

Copyright © 2005 by Imprint Publishing Systems Ltd

www.imprintpublishing.co.uk

ISBN: 1-872-035-97 3

First printing January 2005 (2nd Edition).

Contents

Introduction

Welcome to this second edition Standard Grade Modern Studies Revision Guide. You will find a number of sections in the book, which cover various aspects of the course.

In the first section, you will find summary notes on the most important information which is required to answer Knowledge and Understanding questions. If there are any points that you don't understand, or cannot explain fully, you should refer to your class notes/books and/or your teacher.

This section of the book is divided into four parts. In each part you will find a list of possible exam questions. Try to answer the questions. Four developed points would be enough to meet the demands of a Credit question in the exam.

There are sections which cover how to answer exam style questions and how to study effectively. After reading these sections, it would be a good idea to try some timed past paper questions.

The final section of the book covers the concepts of the Standard Grade course. An understanding of these terms will help you to answer Knowledge and Understanding questions.

Good Luck!

Living in a Democracy – The UK

What the SQA says may be tested in the examination

- How candidates are selected and election of MPs, MSPs, councillors and work place representatives.
- Ways in which representatives work on behalf of those they represent.
- Ways in which individuals and groups can participate by voting, campaigning, taking part in political party, pressure group or workplace activity.
- The rights and responsibilities of individuals and groups in a democratic society.

Typical Examination Questions

The UK and Scottish Parliaments

- Explain the advantages of the First Past the Post System or the Additional Member System. (C)
- Why is it important that people should use their vote? (G/C)
- Describe, in detail, ways in which MPs can represent the interests of their constituents. (G/C)
- Apart from voting, in what ways can UK citizens participate in politics? (G/C)
- Why is it difficult for MPs to represent a large number of groups and individuals? (C)
- "The First Past the Post voting system is unfair. It is time to introduce a voting system which would improve the representation of voters." What arguments could be put forward for and against this point of view? (C)
- What arguments could be used to support the view that councillors are the best people to represent the interests of local people? (G/C)
- Describe ways in which women could increase their participation in local and national politics. (G/C)
- Describe ways in which local councillors can represent the people who live in their areas. (G/C)

- Explain the arguments for and against Proportional Representation. (C)
- Describe ways in which a backbench MP can represent his or her constituents in the House of Commons. (C)
- Describe ways in which supporters could help a political party during an election campaign. (G/C)
- For what reasons do many women and ethnic minorities not participate in politics? (G/C)
- In what ways can MSPs represent their constituents inside and outside Parliament? (G/C)
- Explain why women and ethnic minorities are under-represented in the House of Commons. (C)
- Describe ways in which MSPs can draw attention to problems in their area. (G/C)

Trade Unions

- Describe ways in which trade unions represent their members. (G/C)
- Give reasons why some trade union members think that the job of the shop steward is the most important in the trade union. (C)
- Describe ways in which union members can participate in the work of their trade union. (G/C)
- Describe the social and economic factors which have made it difficult for women to participate effectively in trade unions. (C)
- Give reasons why some workers may not wish to use their right to strike. (G/C)
- Explain what rights and responsibilities trade unions have when representing the interests of their members. (G/C)

Pressure Groups

- Describe the rights and responsibilities of pressure groups. (G/C)
- Explain why a member of a pressure group might participate in: a public debate; a public demonstration; lobbying parliament; a media campaign. (G/C)

Participation	**Rights and Responsibilities**	**Representation**
Different ways in which people take part (or don't take part) in politics, trade unions and pressure groups.	In most societies, citizens have rights and responsibilities. In the United Kingdom, different groups and political parties have slightly different ideas about what these rights and responsibilities are.	Ways different representatives are elected and how they look after the interests of the individuals who elected them. Questions may be asked about representation on different levels including MPs, MSPs, councillors and in the work place.

The UK Parliament and the Scottish Parliament

Candidates for election to the UK or Scottish Parliament can either put themselves forward as independents or be selected by a political party to be its representative. Martin Bell was elected as the Member of Parliament (MP) for Tatton in 1997 as an independent. Most candidates are selected by the major parties, giving them a greater chance of success. This is because the party will be able to help fund the campaign and provide people to help campaign for them. Normally, candidates will have been members of the party for several years and have worked as supporters for other candidates. They will have to be on an approved list of candidates, vetted and circulated from party headquarters. They will have been chosen by a selection committee consisting of party members in the constituency.

Elections

Elections are used to elect Members of Parliament (MPs) and Members of the Scottish Parliament (MSPs). MPs are elected for a maximum of 5 years until the following general election then they can stand in another election. MSPs are elected for 4 years. A by-election is held if an MP dies or resigns between elections.

Parties will use a variety of methods to persuade voters to vote for them. This might include canvassing, posters, leaflets, walkabouts, radio and TV broadcasts, and public meetings. The larger political parties have more money to pay for these. This may give them an advantage over smaller parties and independents.

The Westminster Election

The election system used to elect MPs to Westminster is the 'First Past the Post' (FPTP) system. Under this system the country is divided up into 659 constituencies. In each constituency, the candidate who receives most votes will become the MP.

Safe Seat

A constituency where the MP has a very large majority is called a safe seat.

It would take many thousands of voters to switch from voting for John Reid (Lab) to other candidates for the MP to lose his seat.

Hamilton North and Bellshill (2001)	
Electorate 53,539	Turnout 30,405 (56.79%)
Reid, J (Labour)	18,786 (61.79%)
Stephens, C (SNP)	5,225 (17.19%)
Frain Bell, B (Con)	2,649 (8.71%)
Legg, K (Lib Dem)	2,360 (7.76%)
Blackall, S (SSP)	1,189 (3.91%)
Mayes, S (Soc Lab)	195 (0.64%)
Lab Majority	**13,561**

Marginal Seat

A constituency where the MP has a very small majority is called a marginal seat.

Peter Duncan was elected as the MP because he received more votes than any other candidate, albeit with a very narrow majority. Note, however, that more people voted against him than for him (12,148 + 7,258 + 3,698 + 588 = 23,692 against 12,222 for Peter Duncan).

Galloway and Upper Nithsdale (2001)	
Electorate 52,756	Turnout 35, 914 (60.08%)
Duncan, P (Con)	12,222 (34.03%)
Fleming, M (SNP)	12,148 (33.83%)
Sloan, T (Lab)	7,258 (20.21%)
Wallace, N (Lib Dem)	3,698 (10.30%)
Harvey, N (SSP)	588 (1.64%)
Con Majority	**74**

Selecting Candidates

Who can be a candidate?
✓ A British citizen who is 21 years old or over.
✓ Nominated by 10 electors living in the constituency.
✓ Able to pay a deposit of £500 (returned if the candidate gets 5% of the votes cast).

Who cannot be a candidate?
✗ Members of the Royal Family.
✗ Members of the House of Lords.
✗ Judges, police officers, members of the clergy and civil servants.
✗ Those serving 12 months or more in prison.
✗ Those certified insane.
✗ Undischarged bankrupts.

Electing MPs

Who can vote?
✓ British citizens (including people who have lived overseas for less than 20 years).
✓ 18 year olds and over.
✓ Those on the electoral roll in the constituency.

Those entitled to vote are called the **electorate**.

Who cannot vote?
✗ Members of the Royal Family.
✗ Members of the House of Lords.
✗ Those serving 12 months or more in prison.
✗ Those certified insane.

Voting is not compulsory. Normally, over 70% of the electorate vote in a General Election however, in 2001, only 59% of voters actually voted. This is called **the turnout**. (In local council elections, the turnout may be as low as 30% to 40% of the electorate.)

How to Vote

Voters should check their your name is on the **electoral roll**. Several days before the election, voters will be sent a **polling card**. On it is their name, number on the electoral roll, the date of the election and **the polling station** where to vote.

The polling station – usually a local school, community centre or hall – is open between 7am and 10pm on general election and by-election days.

On election day, the voter takes the polling card to the polling station and shows it to the **polling clerk** who will check the name is on the electoral roll and will give out a **ballot paper**. This will have the names and parties of the candidates printed on it.

The voter takes the ballot paper into a **polling booth** and marks his/her choice with a cross. They then fold the ballot paper and put it in a **ballot box**. Since no other person can see how the voter has voted, it is called a **secret ballot**. The ballot boxes are then collected at 10pm and taken to a central location to be counted.

The winner of the general election will be the party which wins most seats in Parliament. The winner of the 2001 election was the Labour Party.

The 2001 General Election Result

Number of MPs	
Conservative	166
Labour	413
Liberal Democrats	52
Others	28
Total	**659**

First Past the Post System

All electoral systems have advantages and disadvantages.

✓ Advantages of the 'First Past the Post' system:

- voters vote for a single candidate;
- a clear link between the MP and constituents;
- strong government because there is usually one party in control (no coalition);
- a simple system to understand and operate.

✗ Disadvantages of the 'First Past the Post' system:

- difficult for small parties to gain any power;
- many votes are wasted;
- some people think that it gives governments too much power;
- there is nothing for second place. It is 'winner takes all';
- some parties win a greater number of seats than their proportion of the vote would lead you to expect. In 2001, Labour had 63% of the MPs but only 42% of the vote.

Elections to the Scottish Parliament

The first election to the Scottish Parliament since 1707 was held on the 6th May 1999. 129 MSPs were elected, using a new electoral system. This system gave the voter two votes. The first vote was for a constituency MSP. The country was divided into 73 constituencies, each with a choice of candidates to vote for. The person who received most votes was the winner.

However, the second vote was very different. Under this part of the electoral system, people had to vote for a Regional or List MSP. They were given a list of candidates for each party and had to decide which party they wanted to vote for. This system was used to try to ensure that there was a closer link between the percentage of votes and percentage of seats won by each party. The intention was to make it more proportional than the 'First Past the Post' system.

Results from the 2003 Election to the Scottish Parliament

Political Party	Constituency MSPs	List MSPs	Total MSPs
Scottish Labour Party	46	4	50
Scottish National Party	9	18	27
Scottish Conservative and Unionist Party	3	15	18
Scottish Liberal Democrats	13	4	17
Scottish Green Party	0	7	7
Scottish Socialist Party	0	6	6
Scottish Senior Citizens Party	0	1	1
Independents	2	1	3

All electoral systems have advantages and disadvantages. However, the system used for the Scottish Parliament was designed to combine the advantages of 'First Past the Post' and proportional respresentation. This is called the 'Additional Member System'.

✓   Advantages of this system:

- greater likelihood of a coalition government. The Labour Party and the Liberal Democrats formed a coalition government after the 1999 and 2003 elections. This gave some power to the smaller party and reduced the power of the bigger party;
- fewer votes are wasted than under the simple FPTP;
- a strong link between constituency MSPs and voters;
- the number of MSPs from each party should be more in line with the percentage of votes received.

Votes and Seats – The 2003 Scottish Parliament Election

Political Party	% of Votes	% of Seats
Scottish Labour Party	32	39
Scottish National Party	22	21
Scottish Conservative and Unionist Party	16	14
Scottish Liberal Democrats	13	13
Others	5	2
SSCUP	1	1
Scottish Socialist Party	6	5
Green Party	6	5

✗   Disadvantages of this system:

- friction between list MSPs of one party and constituency MSPs of another;
- no strong government, as there is likely to be a coalition (Labour/Liberal Democrat coalition after the 1999 and 2003 elections);
- no clear link between list MSP and constituents;
- many people find it difficult to understand;
- the second vote puts too much power in the hands of the parties, at the expense of individual candidates.

Proportional Representation (PR)

There are many other types of electoral system. However, some are very complicated. The most straightforward form of PR to understand is the 'Party List' system. Under this system, each party puts forward a list of candidates for that party in a particular area. The people in that area then vote for the party of their choice.

The votes for that area are then calculated. Each party will then be allocated a percentage of the seats available in that area, related to the percentage of the votes received. The percentage of seats won will be very close to the percentage of votes.

Thus, if Labour obtained 40% of the vote, they would receive about 40% of the available seats. If there were 10 seats available, this would mean they would get 4 of the seats. For example, the Labour Party might have a list of 10 candidates like the one below. The higher up the list a candidates name appears, the greater chance he or she has of being elected.

1.	Derek Dunsmore	6.	Clair Millar
2.	Martin Kidd	7.	Kate Ferguson
3.	Andrew Kerr	8.	Callum Saunders
4.	Sarah Minto	9.	Philipa Jones
5.	Amber Pattullo	10.	Justine Rafferty

The 40% vote would result in the first four names being elected. The other parties would also go through the same process.

✓   Advantages of this system:
- more chance of a coalition government which would give some power to the smaller parties;
- few votes would be wasted;
- the number of representatives would be close to the percentage of votes received;
- quite easy to understand.

✗   Disadvantages of this system:
- many people think that coalition governments can be weak;
- poor link between the voters and the representatives;
- the list system gives too much power to candidates of large parties. Independent candidates are disadvantaged.

What rights and responsibilities do individuals and groups have in a democratic society?

Rights	Responsibilities
The right to vote (if you are over 18). The right to free speech. This means that you can support or criticise the government. The right to join an organisation and campaign for a particular issue. The right to choose or not to choose a religion. The right to protest. The right to a fair trial.	To turn out and vote. To respect the rights of others to free speech. To work for a political party or pressure group in a peaceful way. To respect other people's rights to choose or not to choose a religion. To protest within the law. To work within the law.

How can people take part (participate) in the political process?

◆ voters can make sure their name is on the electoral roll and vote in local elections and elections for the UK and Scottish Parliaments;

◆ people can join a political party, become involved in making decisions in the constituency, be involved in selecting candidates and help the party campaign during elections;

◆ people can stand as a candidate;

◆ individuals can join a pressure group and try to influence representatives to make decisions in their favour;

◆ people can apply to join a political party and, if accepted by the local constituency, can attend meetings and pay the subscriptions;

◆ constituency party members might be elected to, or invited to join, the local selection committee which will interview prospective candidates and choose the party's candidate for the next election;

◆ after time and much work, individuals might put themselves forward as a candidate for a political party. They will be interviewed and, if selected, the party will find the cash for the deposit, nominees for their nomination paper, funds and helpers for their election campaign.

◆ an individual can become an 'independent' candidate for election but will have to organise and fund their own campaign and pay their own deposit. They are almost certain to lose the deposit, especially in urban areas. They are also unlikely to be elected.

◆ people can help campaign for a candidate in an election by:
  - *putting posters in a house window or car;*
  - *helping to write election material and post or deliver these by hand;*
  - *attending public meetings to support a candidate or to criticise opponents;*
  - *touring the streets with loudspeakers to bring attention to a candidate;*
  - *helping a candidate get items in the local newspapers;*
  - *writing letters of support for a candidate and party to the press.*

How do representatives look after the interests of their constituents in Parliament?

There are many methods representatives can use to put forward the views of their constituents. Inside the House of Commons, MPs can:

◆ take part in debates;
◆ ask questions at Question Time;
◆ call for an adjournment debate;
◆ introduce a Private Member's Bill;
◆ lobby other MPs to support them;
◆ take part in Committee work;
◆ introduce bills under the 10 minute rule.

Inside the Scottish Parliament, MSPs can:

◆ debate and discuss in committees;
◆ check proposed new laws;
◆ question a Minister;
◆ speak in debates;
◆ put forward motions for debate;
◆ suggest amendments to motions;
◆ question the First Minister.

How do representatives look after the interests of their constituents outside parliament?

MPs and MSPs can represent their constituents outside Parliament by:

◆ attending meetings and events;
◆ writing letters/e-mails;
◆ visiting people;
◆ lobbying other influential people to support them;
◆ holding surgeries where members of the public can ask questions.

How representative are our MPs/MSPs?

Do our representatives come from a cross section of society? The short answer to this question is 'no'.

You have much more chance of being elected if you are white, middle class, middle aged and male.

However, it would be fair to suggest that there have been some major improvements in recent years.

The Scottish Parliament has one of the highest proportions of female representatives in the European Union. Of the 129 MSPs, 51 (39.5%) are female.

Female MSPs by party (2003)		
Party	Number	Percentage
Scottish Labour Party	28	56
Scottish National Party	9	33
Scottish Conservative and Unionist Party	4	22
Scottish Liberal Democrats	2	12
Scottish Green Party	2	29
Scottish Socialist Party	4	67
Ind/Other	2	n/a

There are 659 MPs in the House of Commons. In 1983, there were 23 females. This increased to 118 in 2001. However, this only accounts for about 18% of the available seats.

The percentage of women councillors elected in council elections 1992-2003					
Party	1992	1994	1995	1999	2003
Labour	21	16	23.7	21.8	21
SNP	29	18	19.9	24.0	25
Lib. Dem.	29	23	28.5	32.3	32
Conservative	26	23	26.8	23.1	24
Ind/other	19	16	13.0	15.7	15
Total	**22**	**17**	**22.3**	**22.6**	**n/a**

In the 2003 local government elections in Scotland, 1222 councilors were elected. 269 were female and 953 were male. In 1999, 946 male and 276 female councillors were elected. More women are putting themselves forward as candidates – there were 1048 in 2003, an increase of 131 since 1995.

Why do women tend to be under-represented?

Many women don't participate in politics for social and economic reasons.

◆ They may be expected to carry out the traditional duties of women in the home. They find it difficult to find the free time to participate in politics.
◆ Political parties tend to be male dominated. Thus, women may be intimidated when they go to meetings.
◆ Many party members have stereotyped views of

some women. This means that they may think that they don't have the confidence necessary to stand for election. If they do pick women candidates, it is often in seats where there is little chance of winning.
◆ If they have families, it is very difficult for women to find time to participate. This is because many of the meetings are in the evening. The Westminster Parliament often meets very late and many women may find it expensive to pay for a childminder to look after the children.

Why are ethnic minority groups under-represented?

◆ Ethnic minorities in the UK have maintained strong cultural identities. Participation in the democratic process has been slow to develop, resulting in few role models.
◆ Political parties are very often white dominated. Ethnic minority party members may be intimidated when they first go to meetings.
◆ Some parties may have members with racist views. Therefore, they may not pick ethnic minority candidates. When they do pick them, it is often in seats in which they have little chance of winning.
◆ Some voters may have racist views. If a candidate from a different ethnic background stands for election, it is possible some voters may not vote for them.

Why are people with disabilities under-represented?

◆ Sometimes there are insufficient facilities for disabled people to participate in the political process, e.g., access to buildings and limited facilities in meetings. This should change with the building of the new Scottish Parliament at Holyrood.
◆ There are very few disabled MPs, e.g., Anne Begg MP for Aberdeen South, Jack Ashley (now Lord Ashley in the House of Lords) who is deaf and David Blunkett who is blind. Constituency parties may mistakenly not select candidates with a disability because they fear the electorate will only see the person's disability and think they are not capable of doing the job.

Why should people vote?

Parliament is the supreme law-making institution in the United Kingdom, it is responsible for the raising and spending of taxes and can decide whether or not the country goes to war. The Scottish Parliament also makes important laws on health, education and other major aspects of Scottish life. Local authorities decide what to spend on services such as cleansing, education and libraries. If you live in a democracy, you are given the right to vote. This should ensure that a majority of people get a government which runs the country in a way that will respond to their priorities. With this right comes the responsibility to ensure that the right is used. If we do not vote, we may end up with a government which doesn't make the appropriate decisions. If we do not use our right to vote, we can't really complain when the government goes against our wishes.

Rights and responsibilities in a democracy

◆ If we do not carefully guard our freedom of speech and support the rights of others to speak out, even if we disagree with what they say, we could lose it.
◆ It is our responsibility to obey the laws passed by our representatives even when we disagree with them. If we choose to disobey a law then we must be aware that there may be consequences such as a fine or imprisonment.
◆ It is the responsibility of the elected majority to respect the views and wishes of the minority.

Are representatives able to represent the views of all the voters in an area?

Sometimes it is difficult for a representative to look after the interests of all the people in an area. They have to think about the interests of their party, the interests of the country and the interests of the people in an area. For example, if the government is planning to build a nuclear power station in Dumfries, some people might argue that it was in the interest of the country to produce more electricity. The people in the constituency might argue that nuclear power is dangerous and they don't want a power station in their area. The local party may also be against nuclear power. It is obvious from this example that a representative cannot please all of the people all of the time. An MP's/ MSP's/ local councillor's own conscience, views and beliefs will affect the way he/she votes on any issue. However, there are a number of other factors which will influence his/her decisions.

◆ The constituents – The people he/she represents will want the representative to put forward their views.
◆ The constituency party – The members of the local party who did the work of supporting the representative in the election will want him/her to follow their ideas on various issues.
◆ The parliamentary party/council party – The collective views of party backbench representatives in the House of Commons/council chambers may influence the representative.
◆ The Whip System – Representatives are usually elected as the members of a party not as individuals. They must vote for what the party promised in the manifesto. The party leaders expect support from representatives for the tactics employed to promote party policy.
◆ The Media – Newspapers, TV and radio can influence the electorate and put pressure on representatives.

◆ Lobbying – Companies, trade unions, charities, other pressure groups and individuals seek to influence MPs, MSPs and councillors by providing information and writing letters.

Trade Unions

What are trade unions?

Trade unions are organisations which try to protect the rights of workers. They try to ensure that workers are properly represented, that they receive reasonable wages, that they work in a safe and clean environment, that all workers have the same rights and that workers are entitled to holidays every year.

A trade union will talk to an employer about:

◆ pay;
◆ number of hours worked – short-time working leads to reduced take-home pay;
◆ overtime pay;
◆ health and safety at work;
◆ saving jobs;
◆ redundancy pay – 'the sack' is a major threat;
◆ proper training for its members at work;
◆ equal pay for men and women;
◆ equal opportunities for promotion for men, women, ethnic minorities and workers with disabilities;
◆ bullying at work.

Trade unions do this in a number of ways:

◆ Negotiate – try to convince management to make concessions. If an agreed settlement cannot be reached, agree reluctantly to accept the offer or go to arbitration.
◆ Overtime ban – members refuse to work more than their normal hours.
◆ Go slow – members deliberately take more time to do a job than is needed.
◆ Strike – all union members are advised to stop working. This can hurt employers who lose profits and employees who lose wages.

What action can managements take?

◆ Negotiate a settlement.
◆ Try to convince the union representatives that their case is not justified.
◆ Communicate with workers rather than the representatives – appeal to workers by letter or by advertisements in the newspapers that the deal being offered is a fair one.
◆ Propaganda – try to convince the union members there is a 'drift back to work'.
◆ Short time working – hours can be reduced and so pay is reduced.

◆ Redundancy – the sack is the major threat when unemployment is high.

Why do some workers not join a trade union?

◆ many workers think unions are not needed as wages and conditions are satisfactory;
◆ some workers are politically opposed to trade unions;
◆ some workers are in industries which are hard to organise;
◆ some workers take the advantages won by union members without joining the union and contributing to it, e.g., take wage rises but do not pay the union subscriptions;
◆ some employers refuse to deal with unions.

How do trade unions represent the interests of their members?

As trade unions have many members (some unions such as Unison have more than 1,000,000 members), they are able to work for better rights for all workers. If management disagrees with the requests of one worker, they could easily ignore him/her. However, it is more difficult to ignore large numbers of workers who are represented by a union.

Unions are also able to employ specialists, such as financial advisers and lawyers, who can work to protect the interests of the members of the union.

When trade unions work together under the Trade Union Congress (TUC), they are also able to influence the government on issues such as the minimum wage, pensions and the single currency. This helps to ensure a reasonable standard of living for members. Finally,

unions are able to represent the interests of members by negotiating with employers to ensure fair wages and good working conditions.

Trade unions have an important role to play in a democracy. The structure of a trade union gives members the opportunity to participate in decision making.

Union members have the right to elect a number of representatives who make decisions on their behalf. They vote for a shop steward at local level. At national level, they elect a national/executive committee which runs the union. Union members are elected to represent their fellow members at the annual conference.

The national executive and general secretary are elected by the members to carry out policy decided by the annual conference. They represent the members in national negotiations on pay and conditions.

How are trade union representatives elected?

In the past, most union representatives were elected at mass meetings at which voting was carried out by a show of hands. However, many people thought that this was not a fair way (undemocratic). In the 1980s and 1990s, the government introduced laws which forced unions to change. Elections must now be by secret ballot. This should help to avoid intimidation and give people time to think about their vote.

All union officials must stand for re-election on a regular basis. This is designed to ensure that all representatives follow the wishes of the workers.

Why are shop stewards important officials of any union?

Shop stewards are important officials because they rep-

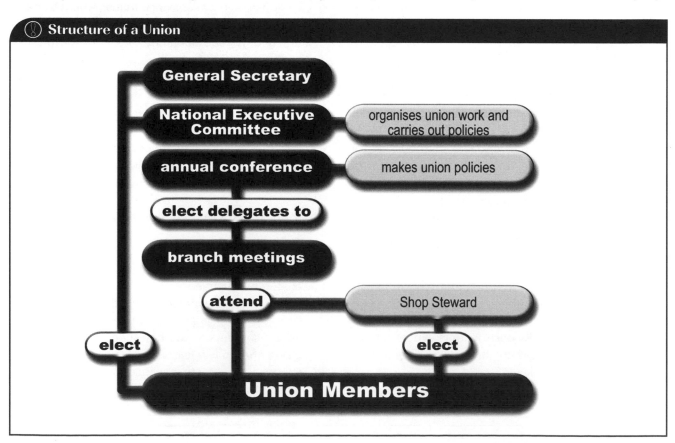

resent the interests of members in the workplace. They will work directly with managers to solve any difficulties. They are also important because:

◆ They will usually recruit new members. If unions don't have members, they will have little power or money.
◆ They are the first people that members will talk to about problems such as health and safety issues or wage increases. If the member doesn't trust the shop steward then he/she may lose faith in all trade unionism.
◆ They are responsible for organising meetings, informing members and conducting ballots. Without this, unions would not be democratic.
◆ They will have to protect the rights of members if they get into disputes with management. If they do this well, workers will get a fair hearing.

How can members participate in the work of a trade union?

There are many ways in which the members can take part in the work of the union. The more the members participate, the more effective the union will be.

Methods of participating

◆ attending meetings (local and national);
◆ voting;
◆ putting their views forward;
◆ writing letters (to representatives such as MPs, MSPs or councillors, newspapers and management);
◆ taking part in industrial action such as a go-slow, a strike, a work to rule, a picket or a demonstration;
◆ putting themselves forward to be a shop steward.

What are the social and economic factors which have made it difficult for women and ethnic minorities to participate effectively in trade unions?

◆ **Social factors which help to explain the under-representation of women.**
Some unions were male dominated in the past. This may mean that women are intimidated and therefore don't participate in the activities of the union. Males may also have traditional attitudes about women. This may mean that they will not vote for women if they stand for election. Many women may also find it difficult to attend meetings because of the timing. Many meetings take place after working hours and there may be more pressure on working women to return home to look after children.

◆ **Economic factors which help to explain the under-representation of women.**
As many women only work part-time, they may feel that there is no point in participating in union activity. They might argue that this is more for full-time workers, who have much more to gain by taking part. Many women also work in low paid employment. This may mean that they can't afford to stay on for meetings, as it will cost them extra money to pay for a childminder. This may also stop them from joining a union in the first place, as they can't afford to pay the membership fees.

◆ **Social factors which make it more difficult for ethnic minorities to participate effectively in unions.**
Many people from ethnic minority backgrounds do not participate in the activities of the unions because they face discrimination. Some members of ethnic minorities have often found it difficult to make progress in unions dominated by white people, some of whom may hold racist views. This may mean that members of ethnic minorities are intimidated when they first go to a union meeting. They may feel that there is little point in attending.

◆ **Economic factors which make it more difficult for ethnic minorities to participate effectively in unions.**
Ethnic minorities are more likely to work in low paid jobs than whites. Low paid workers often don't participate because some can't afford to pay the union subscriptions or are afraid of reduced wages through industrial action or even losing their job. If they are not members then it is difficult for them to participate.

Why do some workers not use their right to strike?

Some workers do not wish to go on strike because they fear that it will stop them from doing their job properly. Some teachers will not go on strike because it may damage the education of children. Some doctors and nurses refuse to strike because it may damage the health of patients.

Other workers do not use their right to strike because they have signed a 'no-strike' agreement with their employers and, if they were to go on strike, they might be dismissed. They may also fear intimidation.

Finally, other workers do not wish to strike because they will not get paid. If they don't get paid, some people may find it difficult to pay the bills.

Rights of trade union members

◆ to join a trade union;
◆ to participate in election of shop stewards and union officials;
◆ to participate in making the policy for their union;
◆ to be kept informed of what their union is doing for them;
◆ to be represented by the union if they are having problems with the management;
◆ to be able to speak freely on any matter.

Responsibilities of trade union members

◆ to pay their union dues;
◆ to speak out if they disagree with something the union wants to do;
◆ to attend union meetings and read the leaflets that their union sends them;
◆ to vote in the elections for shop stewards and union officials;
◆ to vote to decide union policy and to support union policy;
◆ to support their fellow union members;
◆ to report problems to their shop steward or union official.

Ways in which trade union members can participate

◆ join a trade union.
◆ pay union dues;
◆ attend union meetings;
◆ vote in union elections;
◆ stand for election as shop steward or union delegate;
◆ support union policies;
◆ report problems to the shop steward.

What are the rights and responsibilities of trade unions when representing the interests of their members?

Rights

◆ Trade unions have the right to protest if they are unhappy with pay and conditions.

◆ Trade unions have the right to recruit new members.

◆ Trade unions have the right to be consulted over significant changes in the work place.

◆ Trade unions have the right to inform members changes.

Responsibilities

◆ Trade unions have the responsibility to protest in a fair way and within the law.

◆ Trade unions have the responsibility to represent new members and not bully people into joining.

◆ Trade union leaders have the responsibility to listen to their members' wishes and not just to act in their own interests.

◆ Trade unions have a responsibility to keep all members informed.

Pressure Groups

What is a pressure group?

A pressure group is an organisation which attempts to influence the people in power, governments, councils. Examples of pressure groups would include Oxfam; Greenpeace; Save the Children.

What methods do pressure groups use?

Most groups use a combination of the following:

- writing letters or emails (to representatives; newspapers; influential people);
- producing web-site for information;
- lobbying elected representatives;
- demonstrations;
- petitions;
- blockades;
- strikes;
- leaflets;
- posters;
- adverts;
- phone calls;
- meetings;
- publicity stunts.

In a democratic society, people have a responsibility to work within the law. Pressure groups are unelected, often unrepresentative and unaccountable. Some also sometimes break the law and may also use violent methods.

What rights and responsibilities do pressure groups have?

In a democratic society, pressure groups have many rights. However, with these rights come a number of responsibilities. All groups have the right to criticise governments or other bodies but they must try to ensure that all arguments are presented in good faith.

They will also have the right to meet and protest. However, the protest should be peaceful and within the law. Local bodies must also be informed of their wish to protest.

Finally, pressure groups have the right to make other people aware of problems but, at the same time, they must try to ensure that their arguments are sincere and that people are not intimidated into supporting them.

Types of Pressure

Sometimes pressure groups attempt to persuade MPs to take action in the interests of that pressure group. They do this in a number of ways.

- Write letters to the MP, MSP or councillor.
- Petitions, demonstrations, letters to the press will put pressure on an MP, MSP or councillor.
- Put their views to MPs, MSPs or councillors in their surgeries.
- Lobby the MP, MSP or councillor in Parliament or council chamber (with as much publicity as possible).
- Employ professional lobbyists to influence MPs, MSPs or councillors.

Changing Society – The UK

What the SQA says may be tested in the examination

◆ The needs of the elderly in the areas of health, care and shelter. Why some elderly people do better than others in these areas.

◆ How differences in wealth, status and life-chances affect citizens in relation to income and work.
The influence of new technology on the elderly and working population.
How individuals, family groups, local and national government, voluntary organisations and private business may help to meet the needs of the working population and the elderly.
The needs of the unemployed.

Typical Examination Questions

The Elderly

Why do older people make greater use of medical services than people in other age groups? (G/C)
Explain how new technology has helped to meet the personal needs of older people. (C)
Explain why residential care is often the best way to meet the needs of elderly people. (G/C)
What social and economic factors cause some elderly people to have a higher standard of living than others? (C)
What arguments could be put forward to suggest that government should do less, and families do more, to meet the needs of the elderly? (C)
Describe ways in which houses can be adapted to meet the needs of the elderly. (G)
Why are some elderly people wealthier than others? (G/C)
Describe two ways in which the needs of the elderly can be met by voluntary organizations. (G)

◆ Explain why some elderly people have greater health needs than other elderly people. (C)
Explain why some people think that the government should increase the level of the old age pension. (C)

◆ Explain why some elderly people in the UK live in housing which does not meet their needs. (C)

The Working Population and the Unemployed

◆ Describe two ways in which the policies of the Labour government try to help the unemployed and people in low paid work. (G)

◆ In what ways has new technology led to greater job opportunities for some people but not for others? (C)

◆ Describe two ways in which the government helps young people to find jobs. (G)

◆ Give reasons why women who are lone parents might find it difficult to get jobs. (G)

◆ Describe ways in which the policies of the Labour government have helped unemployed people to meet their needs. (G/C)

◆ In what ways has new technology benefited some workers more than others? (C)

◆ What are the arguments for and against a National Minimum Wage. (G/C)

◆ Give two reasons why some lone parents may be unable to enter full-time work. (G)

◆ What arguments could be put forward to support or oppose the view that the government should provide less help and that individuals and families should do more to help the long-term unemployed? (C)

The Family

◆ Give reasons why some families are better off than others. (G)

◆ Give reasons to explain why some families receive more financial help from the government than other families do. (G/C)

◆ Why do families with young children not all have the same standard of living? (G/C)

◆ Why do people with young children have limited job opportunities? (G/C)

◆ Why do some families receive more financial aid from the government than others? (G/C)

◆ What arguments could be put forward to support or oppose the view that the government should provide less help and that individuals and families should do more to help single parent families? (C)

Equality
Differences exist within and between societies. It is important that you know why these differences exist and how they are measured. You could be asked about inequalities in the UK (including the elderly, the employed and the unemployed and families).

Ideology
People have different views about the best way to provide for the needs of all people.

Need
All humans have needs to satisfy. You need to be aware of these needs, differences in the ways they are satisfied, how they change, how they are met by the government, the community and individuals and the extent to which views vary about this.

The Elderly

Who are the 'elderly'?

The basic definition of 'the elderly' relates to the age at which people qualify for a State Retirement Pension, the 'Old Age Pension'. This age is 60 for women, 65 for men, though it will be 65 for both by 2020. Most people have to retire at 65. There are exceptions to the rule, mostly related to some professions and to self-employment.

Physical needs

- mobility;
- eyesight and hearing;
- keeping warm.

Mobility

- Illnesses such as arthritis and rheumatism prevent some elderly people from getting about.
- At age 65+, only one person in six has a licence to drive. Very few own cars due to failing health or the cost. Many have always used public transport.
- Access to public transport can be a problem. Getting to the bus stop and getting on and off a bus with high steps can be a problem.
- Some bus services have been cut.
- Extreme winter temperatures make it difficult for the elderly to move far outdoors or wait in the cold for transport.
- Nearly half the population of those over 85 cannot leave the house alone.
- Safety in the home can be a problem – falling, slipping and dropping things.
- As people get older, diseases can become more crippling and people more infirm. 31% of those aged 85+ cannot get up and down stairs, 7% cannot go to the toilet or get in and out of bed unassisted.

Eyesight and hearing

- Nearly everyone over 65 has to wear glasses. 1 in 5 have eyesight problems even with glasses. This rises to nearly half of those over 85.
- This means that large numbers of the elderly will not be able to read newspapers or books very easily.
- Many will not be able to write to their friends or read letters from their family. This can cause frustration and isolation.
- People who are hard of hearing will not be able to enjoy their TV or radio unless it is turned up so high that it annoys the neighbours. This can lead to ill-feeling between neighbours.

Keeping warm

Keeping warm in winter is more important for older people than most other groups in society. Old people do not know when they are losing heat and, if their body temperature drops too low, they can die from hypothermia.

The death rate increases by 26% for people over 80 during the winter.

Alzheimer's disease

This is also called senile dementia. It is caused by a rapid loss of brain cells and results in major behaviour changes.

It causes physical, emotional and intellectual deterioration in the sufferer - incontinence, verbal abuse and occasional violence towards loved ones and carers; memory loss, with sufferers not recognising close friends and family; inability to carry out the simplest and most basic functions like eating, drinking and dressing.

Puts a major strain on families - 80% of sufferers stay at home. Can lead to feelings of anger and guilt in carers and to family breakdown in many cases.

Emotional needs

- loneliness;
- depression;
- loss of memory;
- boredom;
- insecurity and fear.

Loneliness

Of those people over 75, more than half live alone. 80% of this group are women. Women on average live longer than men.

Depression

Loss of a lifelong partner, living alone, failing faculties, loss of interest in previous activities: all of these can lead to depression in the elderly.

Loss of memory

As people grow older, brain cells die and are not replaced as quickly. Some lose memory rapidly (see Alzheimer's disease). Memory loss may also depend on lifestyle, e.g., heavy drinkers kill many more brain cells. People who retain an active lifestyle may have reduced memory loss.

Boredom

People who have limited interests outside their work will find it difficult to adjust to retirement. Also, as eyesight or mobility begins to deteriorate, people might not be able to do things they enjoyed doing previously, e.g., reading, walking, dancing and cycling.

Insecurity and fear

Society has apparently become more violent. This worries many elderly people who are afraid to leave their homes. Indeed, many fear they will be attacked or robbed in their own homes.

Financial needs

Elderly people face major changes in their lifestyles as a result of retirement. When they retire, most elderly people have a reduced income and therefore cannot afford those things they did when in work.

Equality in Retirement

Physical equality

The elderly face life with varying degrees of fitness. Some enjoy good health having looked after themselves all their lives with a good diet and appropriate exercise. Others are unfit and do not look after themselves.

Some elderly people can afford good health with access to more rapid and appropriate medical treatment, e.g., a private hip replacement operation within weeks of finding it necessary as opposed to waiting months on the NHS.

As people grow older, the body begins to deteriorate. Bodies deteriorate at different rates. Therefore, there are great inequalities in the health of the elderly.

Emotional equality

A major element in physical equality stems from attitude. Some people think themselves old, act accordingly and, as a result, age very quickly. Others take a more positive attitude to age and the ageing process and make more of their abilities - even though they too are not as capable of doing as much as they once did.

Some people give up when they retire. It is as if they feel that once they no longer work, they cease to have any value and their lives are over. This is particularly true of some men. Others see retirement as a challenge and an opportunity to develop.

Some elderly people have a family to sustain them and give their lives some value, e.g., looking after grand-children or giving advice. Others have no partner or family and therefore may have less self-esteem.

This will adversely affect not only their emotional state but will seriously affect their physical state.

Financial equality

There are great inequalities between elderly people and the rest of the population. There are also great inequalities among groups within the population of the elderly.

Financial inequalities between the elderly and the rest of the population

Many elderly people take a drop in their standards of living relative to the general population once they retire. They therefore have to spend a very much higher proportion of their income on the basic necessities of life. Compared to the general population, the elderly are more likely to be poor. 30% of those classed as poor in the UK are elderly.

The elderly as a group own fewer consumer durables such as washing machines, telephones, TVs and DVDs than the general population. Many of them find it very expensive to heat their houses on their low incomes. Others struggle to feed themselves properly.

Financial inequalities between groups of elderly people

There are pensioners who are very well-off when they retire. For a variety of reasons, they have a good income:

◆ they had good jobs with high incomes that enabled them to save a large amount for their retirement;
◆ they have a big occupational pension;
◆ they have invested in a private pension;
◆ they have a wealthy family who help them out.

They are called WOOPIES (well-off older people) or GLAMS (greying, leisured, affluent and married).

Regional inequalities between groups of the elderly

The farther north you travel from London, the more it costs to heat your home and to feed yourself.

As you move northwards, the temperatures are lower for longer in the year and it therefore costs you more to keep yourself warm. This is not taken into account when fixing benefit levels including cold weather payments. This is a means-tested benefit.

The average shopping basket of groceries costs less in the South of England than in Scotland but this is not reflected in pension levels.

Therefore, some elderly are poorer because of the region of the country in which they live.

Means-testing

While most pensioners are entitled to the basic state pension, some are not. They can get Income Support which is means-tested benefit.

To qualify for Income Support, a pensioner will have to make a claim and fill in forms revealing their income and savings. Many pensioners refuse to give this information for reasons of pride and independence or because the forms are complex and confuse them.

Some argue that all payments should be universal, i.e., everyone gets them irrespective of income. Those with higher incomes should then be taxed. Others argue it is up to individuals to provide for their old age. Only the very poor should be targeted for extra help.

Why are the elderly seen by some as a problem?

The number of men and women over retirement age in the UK is growing, both in total and as a proportion of the population. There are now over ten million pensioners. Greater awareness of health issues and improved medication and surgical techniques mean that people are living longer. Some argue that this situation will put a growing financial strain on pensions, the state benefits system, the National Health Service and a whole range of services for the elderly provided by local authorities, charities and other bodies.

The elderly are not a problem!

Many do not accept that one of the richest countries in the world cannot find the resources to give its elderly citizens a much higher level of state pension than they currently enjoy. They point out that the level of pension compares unfavourably with that available to people in other European countries. It is, they say, a simple matter of political priority - fewer nuclear submarines could mean higher pensions.

⚠ Important

The following notes are placed under various headings for convenience, but remember that the issues covered are all very closely linked, especially if you are an older person!

What state benefits are available?

A recent government leaflet listed the following:

◆ Retirement Pension – paid to men at 65 and to women at 60 who have paid National Insurance.
◆ Over 80 Pension – for people who have little or no state pension.
◆ Attendance Allowance – for ill or disabled people who are over 65.
◆ Christmas Bonus – paid every year to over-65s who qualify for the above or for Income Support.
◆ Cold Weather Payment – over 60s can qualify.
◆ Winter Fuel Payment – for over 60s living at home.
◆ Income Support – available but can depend on level of savings.
◆ Housing Benefit – if older people are on a low income. Paid through local council.
◆ Council Tax Benefit – as with Housing Benefit.
◆ Help with health costs – pensioners can get free NHS prescriptions, free NHS dental treatment and free NHS sight tests.
◆ Pension Credit for people aged 60 and over replaces Minimum Income Guarantee.

Despite this apparently long list, representatives of elderly people argue that many of their number are still living in poverty because:

◆ Many older people are not aware of the benefits available.
◆ Many older people see the benefits as 'charity' and are unwilling to claim.
◆ The forms which have to be filled in are complicated and confusing.
◆ Not everyone qualifies anyway.

Who should receive benefits?

Governments face a dilemma as a significant minority of elderly people do not live in poverty. They have to decide whether to target increases in benefits at the most needy, which means that there will be 'means-testing'. 'Means-testing' is when the authorities check up on the income and savings of elderly people. This, for many, is morally unacceptable, particularly where the elderly are concerned.

It also gives rise to unfairness, because wherever the level of benefit entitlement is set, some people will be just above it, and 'miss out'. They will argue that they are being penalised for having 'saved for a rainy day', and that, having paid tax and National Insurance throughout their working lives, they should be entitled to benefits as of right.

Particular difficulties have arisen with regard to house ownership – older people may have little income but may own a house. Should they have to sell it in order to contribute towards the cost of care? This has often become very contentious when elderly citizens have had to move out of their homes and into some kind of residential care.

The alternative is that improved benefits are given to all, including those who don't need them. It should be said that this difficulty arises in the provision of many of the other support services as well.

There was anger at a 75p pension increase in 2000 and demand that pensions should be linked to average earnings. The Chancellor has now undertaken to increase pensions by 2.5% per year.

What other support is available?

Older people are also supported by a range of services and organisations. Local councils are important in this area, as are charities and voluntary organisations. Some of the services and facilities which are often available to older people are listed below. It is important to remember that all of the facilities and services are not necessarily available to every elderly person in every area. The level of support can also vary – most local councils offer cheap fares on public transport but some of the concessions are more generous than others. Many elderly people think that this is unfair.

Where and how can older people receive help/support/company?

◆ Day centres
◆ Lunch clubs
◆ Meals on wheels
◆ Cheap travel
◆ 'Evergreen' clubs
◆ Reduced-price entertainment
◆ Church organisations
◆ Citizens' Advice Bureaus
◆ Welfare Rights Offices
◆ The government, local councils, charities and other voluntary and professional bodies all publish leaflets designed to help older people.

Older people have pressure groups which lobby on their behalf, and which can also offer support and advice:

◆ **Representation in the Scottish Parliament**
'Eleven weeks ago we didn't exist. Now senior citizens at last have a genuine voice in parliament.'
John Swinburne, SSCUP MSP, 2nd May 2003.
John Swinburne MSP was elected as a list member for Central Scotland Region and is the leader (and only MSP) of the Scottish Senior Citizens Unity Party. He received 17,146 second votes, almost 7% of the votes cast.

◆ **National Charities/Pressure Groups**
Age Concern publishes leaflets, including one on combating ageism. Age Concern can also provide 'at home daycare'. Help the Aged publishes a wide range of leaflets on finance, housing and home safety and health. All are available free of charge.

◆ **National voluntary group; National Pensioners' Convention**
This group has successfully lobbied Parliament about the State Retirement Pension.

◆ **Local voluntary groups: Elderly Forum**
These groups often try to get better deals on local transport. They can also keep an eye on their local council's Social Work Department, putting the case for the elderly when budgets are decided.

Health

For older people, the government is aiming to:

- prevent ill-health and promote the independence of older people;
- make sure that the elderly receive the medical or social service they need quickly;
- make sure that older people all get a wide range of services suited to their needs, wherever they live;
- ensure that, if older people have to move from one area to another, the service they receive carries on without a break;
- take into consideration what older people themselves want.

Like the rest of us, older people have access to all the various services of the NHS, though the special situations in which they often find themselves have led to a feeling that the NHS and the social and caring services have not been responsive enough to their needs.

There is also a feeling that medical, social work and other services, which may all be dealing with the same elderly person, have not always kept in close enough touch with one another.

Things have improved!

Health provision for older people has moved forward in many ways in recent years:

- better mobility aids;
- more suitable design of household appliances and fittings;
- 'CareCall' systems in sheltered housing;
- better and more discreet hearing aids;
- 'flu jabs and inhalers;
- free eye tests;
- free prescriptions;
- free NHS dental treatment;
- free NHS wigs/fabric supports;
- help with travel costs to hospital;
- hip replacements;
- less invasive surgical techniques.

What are the current health issues facing older people?

Older members of society tend to be ill more often than their younger fellow-citizens.

It is also claimed that older members of society are not keen to go to the doctor, perhaps allowing a condition to develop. Some say that recent changes in the NHS as a whole have led to practices which affect the elderly more than other sections of society.

These would include:

- less likelihood of home visits by GPs;
- more likelihood of seeing different doctors;
- long waiting times for treatment;
- long trips to hospitals;
- early discharge from hospital.

Typical complaints include deteriorating sight and hearing, deteriorating joints and muscles and diminished mental alertness. Viruses and 'bugs', which younger people shake off, can be fatal to the elderly.

'Care in the Community' policies require that older people, who previously were accommodated in 'bed-blocking' geriatric wards, should be looked after in the community. Since the resources to do this were sometimes not available, the policy placed great strain on medical practices and social services. Less fit older people were, and are, often cared for by partners or other close relatives.

The government has recognised the personal and financial strain which this can place on families. It has moved to support carers, though neither the benefits nor the provision of respite for carers is adequate.

More recently there have been assertions that health authorities were prioritising in favour of younger patients, leaving older people without the treatment they required.

Some health authorities have brought forward proposals to close hospitals or reduce local services as part of their reorganisation of health services. Such proposals have been opposed strongly by groups representing elderly people. Protest marches, demonstrations and lobbying of MPs and MSPs have all been attended by significant numbers of elderly people. Increasingly, politicians will have to pay more attention to the views of elderly people because they are more likely to vote than some other groups.

Scotland is different!

The Scottish Parliament has introduced free personal and nursing care for elderly people - something that is not available to elderly people in England and Wales. The Scottish Executive describe this policy as 'one of devolution's major successes'. However, it has to be recognized that this is a costly policy and it is not certain that free personal and nursing care is available to every elderly person in Scotland who needs this type of support.

Care in the Community

Nursing homes care for those elderly people who need a home with nursing services because they have had strokes or are bedridden.

Community nursing services provide home visits from health visitors and chiropodists.

The local authority housing department adapts the homes of elderly people for wheelchair use or by installing community alarms.

Voluntary organisations work with the local authority (often with funds from the local authority) to provide a range of services for the elderly:

◆ meals on wheels delivers hot dinners to the elderly in their own homes;
◆ day care centres and lunch clubs provide a meeting place, entertainment, warmth, meals and access to advice;
◆ support groups offer help and advice.

Social work departments assess the needs of the elderly and provide services such as:

◆ day care centres and lunch clubs in association with churches and other voluntary organisations;
◆ home helps to help the elderly look after their own homes;
◆ laundry facilities to help the carers of those who are incontinent or for those elderly people who do not have laundry facilities in their own homes;
◆ residential homes which provide care for those who can no longer live on their own even with alarms and home helps;
◆ sheltered housing.

How have pro-elderly groups argued the health case?

They point out that:

◆ society has a moral duty to look after its senior citizens;
◆ health care should be delivered on the basis of need, not economics;
◆ the elderly have paid National Insurance contributions for many years;
◆ age should not come into health care decisions.

Housing

Housing possibilities for the elderly include:

◆ owner-occupation – they own their own house;
◆ renting from a local council;
◆ renting from a housing association;
◆ renting from a private landlord;
◆ living with close relatives in a 'granny flat';
◆ paying for accommodation in a retirement home.

> ### ⓘ Important
>
> **Very few older people really have this range of choice.**

Where do the elderly live?

The majority of older citizens still live in 'normal' housing. There is a view that they are often most comfortable in a house with which they are familiar and that they should be supported in continuing to live there. The

provision of home helps, meals on wheels and health visitors can help with this. For some, however, an alternative to conventional housing is preferable.

What specialised accommodation is available?

Older people who cannot quite manage a 'normal' house can live in:

- amenity housing;
- sheltered housing;
- very sheltered housing;
- a residential home – charitable, private or local authority;
- a nursing home.

 Important

> **The definitions of the above can vary from area to area across Scotland. Don't worry if you think that you haven't heard of a couple of them - they may well just have a different name in your part of the country!**

The demand for specialised housing far exceeds the supply – there are just not enough sheltered houses in some areas.

Older people who wish to transfer from one area of Scotland to another, perhaps to be nearer relatives, can find it very difficult. A suitable house or a place in a residential home may not be available. There may also be arguments between health authorities about who is to pay what.

Housing and health are very closely related. Heating can be inadequate, either because the heating system is poor or because the occupier of the house cannot afford to pay the bills.

There is now a recognition that new housing should be 'barrier- free' – designed in such a way that people can continue to live there for as long as they wish.

The voluntary sector

The voluntary sector provides a variety of services for the elderly. Organisations include:

- Age Concern;
- Help the Aged;
- WRVS;
- Red Cross;
- Churches;
- Salvation Army;
- Alzheimer's Society.

Services provided include:

- fund raising;
- day care centres;
- lunch clubs;
- home visiting services;
- transport – buses and private cars;
- respite care for carers;
- residential homes;
- sheltered housing;
- community alarm services;
- organised holidays.

Family, friends and community

Friends, family and the local community are extremely important sources of help. This help is available to elderly people to varying degrees. Some elderly people get a tremendous amount of help from these sources and others get none at all. It depends on the friends, the family, the community and on the elderly themselves.

The private sector

Private accommodation

Private companies provide services for the elderly for profit. They are mainly involved in housing, nursing homes, retiral complexes and residential care.

Concessionary prices

Some private companies reduce prices for the elderly at times when business is slow. Cheap haircuts, reduced rail fares or bus fares at off-peak times, winter holidays etc. are examples.

Pressure groups

The elderly are an increasingly important pressure group as their numbers continue to grow and as proportionately they become a larger section of society.

Organisations such as Help the Aged and Age Concern spend part of their time acting as pressure groups to help the elderly.

Elderly people use all the methods of pressure outlined in the section on pressure groups.

Ideology

The right-wing view is that the state should only provide help for those in greatest need and that it is the responsibility of individuals and their families to provide for themselves. Services therefore have to be means-tested.

The left-wing view is that services should be provided for everyone (universal benefits) and that individuals and families should provide assistance.

The Working Population and the Unemployed

The working population (28 million people) is made up of:

◆ men aged 16 to 65 years of age;
◆ women aged 16 to 60 (from 2020 it will be the same as men);

and who are:

◆ employed or;
◆ self-employed or;
◆ on training schemes or;
◆ seeking work – the unemployed.

The non-working population (29.5 million people) is made up of:

◆ children up to 16 years of age;
◆ students;
◆ retired people;
◆ those too ill to work;
◆ those who choose not to work.

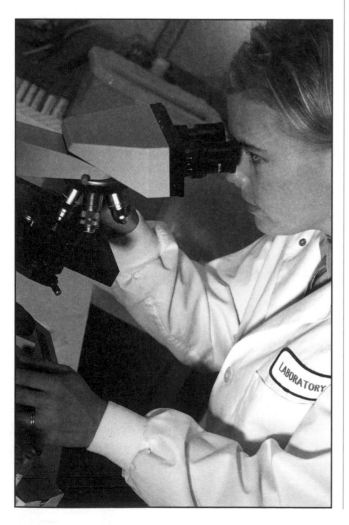

Who are unemployed?

To be described as unemployed you have to be:
◆ out of work;
◆ registered as unemployed;
◆ looking for work;
◆ willing to accept any suitable job you are offered.

Unemployment

Governments have tried, over many years, to minimise unemployment, though there have been disagreements about how this is best achieved. Unemployment can have serious effects on individuals and families:

◆ loss of income;
◆ loss of self-respect;
◆ loss of status, e.g., with banks;
◆ tensions within families;
◆ loss of structured day;
◆ poor mental and physical health;
◆ loss of friends at work - social exclusion?

The country as a whole and governments 'lose out' because:

◆ a valuable economic resource is not being used;
◆ less tax is collected;
◆ more benefit is paid out;
◆ there may be social unrest if large numbers are unemployed;
◆ an 'underclass' may develop;
◆ experienced workers may be lost.

Factors affecting employment and unemployment

Government economic policy

Government economic policies can influence the amount of economic activity. Some economists argue that when governments cut taxes, people have more money to spend. This means that individuals and companies will be able to buy more goods and services or invest money in new enterprises. This type of spending can mean jobs are created.

This will give workers wages and salaries which can create an increased demand for goods.

Supporters of tax cuts argue that, in the longer term, a successful economy means that, although people and businesses are paying lower rates of tax, more tax will be collected as profits and wages are higher.

Some people think that if there are tax cuts then there will be less money for the government to spend on programmes such as building roads or schools. High levels of unemployment will be created because of reduced demand, high interest rates and cutbacks in spending.

Economic factors

◆ people may decide to buy fewer goods and services depending on their personal circumstances;
◆ world recession may reduce the demand for goods;
◆ foreign competition – if other countries make goods and services better or cheaper than us then we will not sell as many products. Unemployment will rise.
◆ decline in traditional industries such as ship-building, engineering and textiles.

New technology

The introduction of new technology has contributed to job losses. However, the new products which have resulted from technological developments have also created jobs.

Advantages of new technology

◆ lower manufacturing costs because fewer workers are employed. This leads to lower prices and more sales.
◆ profits increase leading to more investment and more jobs;
◆ product quality is improved therefore more goods are sold;
◆ new products are developed and manufactured leading to new jobs being created.

Disadvantages of new technology

◆ jobs are taken over by machines;
◆ retraining is often required;
◆ deskilling of many formerly skilled jobs;
◆ new technology is very mobile – for example, call centres can be moved easily from the UK to India resulting in local unemployment.

The needs of the unemployed

Financial needs

◆ Unemployed people need a job to get money so they can have a decent standard of living.

◆ Until they get a job, they need some money to be able to afford the necessities of life such as food, housing and clothes.
◆ 38% of the people living in poverty in west central Scotland come from an unemployed household.
◆ The main reason for people falling into debt is unemployment.

Education and training needs

◆ To get a job, unemployed people may need education and training to learn new skills.
◆ Unemployed people may need to learn job-finding skills such as how to fill in application forms or how best to present themselves at interview.

Emotional needs

◆ When people have been made unemployed or have been unemployed for a long period, they can become depressed or have low self-esteem.
◆ Some have attempted suicide.

Health needs

There is a strong relationship between unemployment, poverty and poor health.

Studies have demonstrated that when people become unemployed, their health deteriorates because of poorer nutrition, colder houses and low self-esteem.

Community needs

When an area suffers from high levels of unemployment, it may go into a spiral of decline. When large numbers of workers are paid off in an area, it has a major negative effect.

◆ skilled people move away;
◆ shops close;
◆ amenities decline, e.g., bus services, libraries;
◆ housing areas deteriorate;
◆ vandalism, drug abuse and crime increase;
◆ public services are reduced;
◆ employers looking to set up new enterprises find the area unattractive and take their new jobs elsewhere;
◆ in extreme cases, community breakdown can lead to rioting and 'no-go areas'.

Equality

Financial inequality: employed and unemployed

Compared with the rest of the community, the unemployed, as a group, suffers from poverty. Studies have shown that two adults and two children living on social security receive an income from the state less than they need for a basic lifestyle. A basic lifestyle means no smoking, drinking, cosmetics, jewellery, annual holiday, freezer, car or Christmas pantomime.

Inequality among the unemployed

The needs of the unemployed are not all the same. Different groups of unemployed workers have different problems to face.

Unskilled workers

Unskilled workers can find it harder to get jobs. Employers will pay off unskilled workers sooner than skilled workers because they know they can find replacements quickly if necessary. Unskilled workers are more likely to suffer from long-term unemployment.

Young workers

After leaving school, young workers have few skills and no experience. They have similar problems to unskilled workers.

Ethnic minority workers

Discrimination against ethnic minorities still exists despite being made illegal by the 1976 Race Relations Act. Some groups of ethnic minority workers still tend to be paid less and suffer higher rates of unemployment than the rest of the population.

Older workers

Many older workers lose their jobs because their skills have been replaced by new technology. It is cheaper to employ someone with less skill to work the new technology.

Older workers may have to retrain to find a new job. Retraining can be expensive, so an employer is more likely to train a younger person who will have a longer working life.

Disabled workers

Disabled workers face prejudice from some employers who argue that their disability will prevent them from working effectively.

It may cost an employer to adapt premises and technology to suit disabled workers. An employer may be unwilling to meet these costs.

Women workers

Some women would like to be able to work but for a number of economic and social reasons are unable to do so.

◆ lack of child care facilities;
◆ family commitments, e.g., caring for an elderly or a disabled relative;
◆ expected to be a housewife;
◆ lack of training and career opportunities;
◆ stopping work to have a family prevents many women from having a career;
◆ discrimination – some employers still do not think women can work as well as men.

Although laws have been passed to stop discrimination against women, many women still feel that they are meeting barriers.

It is also the case that women with children often have to take part-time, low paid jobs which do not leave them any better off and which do not have a career structure.

Long term unemployed

People who have been unemployed for a long time find it difficult to get back into the ways of working. Employers are less likely to employ someone who has not worked for a long time.

Regional unemployment

It is easier to find jobs in some regions of the country than in others.

Unemployment and crime

The government is especially concerned that there may be a link between unemployment and crime and is anxious that young people should be given every opportunity for training and advice.

Some large cities have areas which do not offer good prospects to young people, and these have been targeted. At the same time, young people who choose not to take up any of the government's offers may find that their benefits are affected.

Lone Parents

Lone parents, particularly mothers, are also being given special support. It is recognised that having young children is a barrier to full-time employment, so the government has tried to make more childcare facilities available, while helping lone parents to meet the cost.

Employers have been encouraged to allow job-sharing, part-time working and the use of 'flexi-time' to permit more lone parents to go out to work.

Again, even when lone parents try to enter the job market, they may find that they do not have the up-to-date skills needed to compete with younger people.

Ideology

Although the main political parties agree that unemployment is unacceptable, they have different ideas about how to tackle it.

Labour Party

Labour Party employment policy aims to create the conditions to enable the private sector to flourish and the public sector to modernise. They also emphasise training. They argue that as well as providing the workforce with skills, training promotes equality by giving people a fairer chance to compete for jobs.

Conservative Party

Conservative Party employment policy aims to create the conditions to enable the private sector to flourish. The Conservatives also wish to invest in training and also help areas of high unemployment.

Liberal Democrat Party

Measures for improving the economy to reduce unemployment include a capital investment programme to build roads, schools, hospitals and increased investment in education and training to provide the unemployed with new skills.

Scottish National Party

The SNP claim that full employment in Scotland will only be achieved with independence. They propose investing to stimulate the Scottish economy and increasing spending on infrastructure with rail electrification, road improvement and water and sewerage improvement given priority.

Support for the unemployed

What benefits are available?

Despite regular efforts to make it simpler, the benefits system is still very complicated, and benefit has to be worked out for each individual.

Lone parents

The most important benefits which may be available to lone parents include:

◆ child benefit;
◆ statutory maternity pay or maternity allowance;
◆ housing benefit;
◆ income support;
◆ jobseeker's allowance;
◆ social fund (grants, e.g., maternity costs).

> ⓘ **Remember**
>
> **Not all lone parents will qualify for every one of these benefits.**

Not every lone parent family is badly off. Some lone parents do have well-paid jobs which allow them to afford child care. There is now a growing number of employers who offer helpful maternity arrangements, and anti-discrimination legislation means that not only

are women entitled to Statutory Maternity Pay but their job should also be kept open for them. Yet again, other lone parents are supported by their families, sometimes financially, sometimes in helping with child care.

Over 50s

Over 50s present different problems. Their skills are often out of date, they can be unfairly seen as 'too set in their ways' and employers sometimes overlook experience in favour of youth. Ageism also plays a part in making it difficult for older people to get back into employment. The government has put in place training schemes to update skills and offers financial incentives (e.g. Employment Credit) to those who find work.

The 'New Deal'

In the past, unemployed people seeking support often found the system confusing. For example, they could find that, while they had to go to the Job Centre to get one of the forms they had to fill in, they might have to go to the Post Office or to the local council office for others. Once they had filled them in, it could take ages to get a reply.

The 'New Deal' tries to make things much easier. The government aims to get people off benefits ('Welfare to Work') and to find them 'lasting, worthwhile work'. Although it now covers virtually anyone who is unemployed, it was brought in under three headings, starting in 1998:

◆ New Deal 18-24.
◆ New Deal 25 plus.
◆ New Deal 50 plus.

Examples of ways in which the New Deal tries to help:

◆ an Individual Training Plan from a personal adviser;
◆ the guarantee of high quality work or training;
◆ financial support - possibly New Deal allowance, Housing Benefit, Council Tax benefit, 'top-ups' for lower paid, Employment Credit for over 50s who get a job;
◆ advice on self-employment;
◆ very specialised help, e.g., for young musicians;
◆ support for employers who take on 'New Deal' employees;
◆ possibility of placement with a voluntary organisation;
◆ arrangements to make sure that lone parents are better off in work.

> ⓘ **Important**
>
> **'New Deal' is very wide-ranging, so don't try to memorise all of the details – concentrate on some good examples!**

While the schemes noted have been successful, some people have worried about the pressure on people to take jobs or risk losing their benefit. This can lead, they say, to people being in jobs to which they are not suited, which may be well below their ability level, and which may be 'dead-end'.

The government replies by pointing out that we have a personal, social and family responsibility to work if we are able to.

Examples of how the individual is helped:

◆ Government – financial support through the benefits system – see 'New Deal';
◆ Local council/volunteers – 'job clubs';
◆ Local council/private business – reduced prices for leisure activities;
◆ Government – special training schemes and tax advantages for young people, lone parents, over 50s, long term unemployed;
◆ Private business/government – firms encouraged to allow 'job-sharing'.

How do the authorities attempt to create employment opportunities?

Government, local councils and local enterprise companies work to encourage firms to set up in their areas. They often work together, sometimes using financial support from European Union sources. Certain parts of the country, usually areas which have seen the closure of traditional industries, are targeted. Business parks are often built in advance, so that interested companies can be offered ready-made premises. Roads are often improved to make a site more attractive but the main incentives are usually in the form of money – firms are offered grants to persuade them to start up a local operation.

The government has also recognised that some areas of our country, particularly inner cities, face a range of difficulties, of which unemployment is only one.

Measures which tried to deal only with unemployment in these areas are unlikely to be successful, because the problem of unemployment is so closely linked to other difficulties that they all have to be looked at together.

The life chances available to people living in the inner cities are in great contrast to those available to residents of nearby, well-off suburbs. Generally, inner city babies will grow up to live shorter lives, to live less well, to see more crime, to eat less well, to secure less rewarding jobs and to be ill more often. The government has made money available to tackle poor social and housing conditions, to provide better educational opportunity and to develop health care.

Other measures include steps to combat drug abuse, to reduce crime and to encourage residents to participate in the running of their area.

How successful are these measures?

It is difficult to assess the success of these measures because we don't know how many people would get jobs even if the support mentioned above didn't exist. What can be said is that unemployment has shown a downward trend nationally, though there are still significant pockets of unemployment and social deprivation which are responding much more slowly. Unemployment still hovers around the million mark and many of the jobs which have emerged have been part-time or temporary, low paid, unskilled and lacking a career structure. Some 'call centres' are examples of this. At the same time, some benefit claimants say that they have found claiming more difficult, and have felt that they have been pushed into a 'take it or risk your benefit' situation. Many have benefited from training; others have retrained because they were faced with no choice.

Concern has been expressed that the amount of money spent by enterprise companies has not resulted in a sufficient number of new jobs. There is also a feeling that grants are being given to multinational companies which basically don't need the money. It has also been suggested that having different agencies competing for firms to set up with them doesn't actually create extra jobs - it is really just a costly way of deciding which town gets jobs which were going to be created anyway.

The National Minimum Wage

The Labour government brought in a National Minimum Wage. Supported by trade unions, it was introduced as a matter of social fairness, to lessen the exploitation of workers (particularly women in low-paid jobs), to help free people from the poverty trap and to make it more worthwhile to work, possibly reducing the number of people claiming benefit.

The measure was opposed by the Conservative Party and by many businesses. They argued that it would increase costs and people would be made redundant, especially in small businesses. It was more bureaucratic, prices would go up and unemployment would rise.

Though it is too soon to measure the long-term impact of the National Minimum Wage, these fears do not seem to have been realised. Businesses have geared themselves up to the new situation and many people have benefited.

The Family

Successive governments have tried to emphasise the importance of family relationships. Both the previous Conservative government, and to a lesser extent, the present government, have put emphasis on both the value of the family and 'family values'. This was in response to a public feeling that society was becoming less disciplined and was somehow related to the family unit being less important and having less control over the behaviour of children.

Fear of street crime, for example, seemed to alarm the public even although hard evidence to justify the fear was not always there. Politicians reacted, arguing that stable families lead to a stable society which is in the interest of us all. There are problems with defining 'the family' in a changing society.

The family is still the most common structure in this country and the traditional family still carries strong support. However, it is no longer appropriate to assume that 'the family' will consist of mum, married to dad, and their children. Government ministers have been accused of 'double standards' – trying to persuade the British people that marriage and the family is a good thing while having themselves been in marriages which have broken up.

Governments have a problem. They know that there is still broad support for the institution of marriage. However, they also know that efforts to support it, for example, through the taxation or benefits system, may infringe on the human rights of citizens who live under a different arrangement. On the other hand, the government is also aware that married couples would be up in arms if it appeared that there was a financial penalty in being married.

Remember

Many of the government's measures which are designed to support unemployed citizens, disabled citizens and other disadvantaged groups are also effectively helping and supporting their families. When answering an examination question on 'the family', you can use material you have learned in relation to unemployed people as long as it is relevant to the question you have been asked.

Remember

Usually, when we think of 'the family', we think about parents with very young or school-age children. However, 'the family' can also be, for example, an elderly couple who may be facing very different issues from their younger fellow citizens.

Respite care

One important way in which families can be helped and supported is through 'respite care'. Family members who need a high level of care can be offered, for example, weekends away in suitably adapted accommodation. This benefits the carer, the person being cared for and helps to meet the family's needs. Respite care may be provided by local authorities or charitable/voluntary organizations.

Government support for 'the family'

- ◆ child benefit;
- ◆ statutory maternity/paternity pay;
- ◆ income support;
- ◆ child tax credit;
- ◆ council tax benefit;
- ◆ housing benefit;
- ◆ help with health costs.

Government support for 'the older family'

- ◆ attendance allowance;
- ◆ carer's allowance;
- ◆ community care grants.

Family carers

Looking after a member of the family who needs a high level of support can put great pressure on other family members. While this often involves elderly people, the Scottish Executive has recently recognized that there are also families with younger carers who are under intense pressure. Steps are now being taken to provide such carers with more support. For example, one medical practice recently contacted all its registered patients in an attempt to identify 'hidden carers' in order that they can be provided with any necessary support.

Keeping it together

Organisations such as 'Relate' can offer support to families where relationships are under strain. 'Relate' can try to resolve arguments and disputes which may be threatening to break up the family unit.

The changing face of the British family

- ◆ Attempts to promote marriage as an ideal have met strong opposition – for instance from people who have left unsatisfactory marriages. They feel it is unfair if they are labelled as failures. Some women's groups are particularly concerned about this, pointing out that many women leave a relationship with a violent partner for the good of their children.
- ◆ We live in a multi-cultural Britain – some ethnic groups place very great emphasis on the extended family.
- ◆ Many families are led by lone parents who bring up well-balanced children. Not every traditional family produces useful citizens.
- ◆ Gay and lesbian couples are part of society and some bring up children.

Ideologies

What the SQA says may be tested in the examination.

- The ideologies of the USA or Russia or China.
- The ways in which, and the extent to which, ideology affects equality (see rights and responsibilities in each country).
- The ways and extent to which individuals and groups can participate.
- The ways in which the government responds to dissent.

Questions will cover:

- The USA, Russia and China.

Some questions typical of those you may be asked in the exam.

USA

- Describe how US citizens can influence the government. (G/C)
- Why is the turnout of voters in US elections low? (G/C)
- Why do many African Americans and Hispanic Americans not vote in elections? (G/C)
- How can US citizens participate in politics? (G/C)
- How are the rights of US people protected by the Constitution? (C)
- What are the rights and responsibilities of US citizens? (G/C)
- In what ways does the 'Capitalist economic system' allow many Americans to have a high standard of living? (C)
- What social, political and economic factors explain why many African Americans and Hispanic Americans remain at the bottom of US society? (C)
- Describe ways in which some ethnic minority groups are not treated equally in housing, health, crime, education and the justice system. (G/C)
- Describe the evidence of social inequalities in the USA. (C)
- Why do people want to live in the USA? (G)
- Why have some US citizens made more social and economic progress than others in recent years? (C)

Russia

- How can Russians participate in politics? (G/C)
- What rights do Russian citizens enjoy? (G/C)
- How might these rights allow Russian citizens to improve their living standards? (G/C)
- In what ways are the rights of Russian citizens limited? (G/C)
- What social and economic problems do some Russian citizens now face? (G/C)
- In what ways have the social and political lives of Russian people changed in recent years? (C)
- Why do some Russians have a higher living standard than others? (G/C)
- Describe ways in which national groups within Russia are not treated fairly. (G/C)
- Describe the evidence of social inequalities in Russia. (C)

China

- Why is it difficult for Chinese people to protest against the government? (G/C)
- In what ways can Chinese people participate in politics? (G/C)
- What rights do Chinese citizens enjoy? (G/C)
- In what ways might these rights allow Chinese citizens to improve their living standards? (G/C)
- Why does the Chinese Communist party not allow any opposition to its rule? (G/C)
- In what ways does the Chinese government make sure that Communism is the only political system allowed in China? (G/C)
- Why have China's economic reforms been good for some people and bad for others? (G/C)
- What is the 'one child' policy? (G/C)
- What rights and responsibilities do the Chinese people have? (G/C)
- In what ways are the rights of Chinese citizens limited? (G/C)
- Why do people believe that the economic system of China works well? (G/C)
- Why are some Chinese people better off than others in health, education and housing? (G/C)
- Describe the evidence of social inequalities in China. (C)

Equality
Differences exist within and between societies. It is important that you know why these differences exist and how they are measured. You could be asked about inequalities between different groups in the USA or Russia or China.

Ideology
People have different views about the best way to provide for the needs of all the people. You should have a knowledge about these differences. You should also be aware of different views on the value of human rights, equality and dissent in the USA or Russia or China.

Participation
There are different ways in which people take part or don't take part in politics and pressure groups. You may be asked about different types of participation in the USA or Russia or China.

Rights and Responsibilities
In most societies, citizens have rights and responsibilities. You should have a knowledge of these rights and responsibilities in the USA or Russia or China.

The USA

Who are the Americans?

In many ways, the United States of America is a unique nation. It is a nation of immigrants with people coming from all parts of the world, including Scotland, Ireland, England, Germany, France, Italy, Sweden, China, Mexico, Russia and some countries in Africa.

The ancestors of black or African Americans were originally brought to the US as slaves. Even after the abolition of slavery, they were discriminated against and suffered from segregation in many US states. Discrimination meant it was difficult for African Americans to get decent education, jobs or housing. In the 1960s and 1970s, African Americans thought that, by participating in the political system, they could gain equality and improve their life chances. They managed to get equal rights laws passed but then found themselves still at a social and economic disadvantage to whites.

Traditionally, Hispanic Americans have entered the USA from Mexico, Cuba and Puerto Rico to find work. They have competed with African Americans for the lowest paid jobs in industry and agriculture. They also competed for the lowest cost housing. Consequently, there is a history of violence between the groups in cities like New York.

In the south and south west of the USA, 'wetbacks' – illegal immigrants from Mexico – work in the fields, in sweat shop industries and as family servants. As they are illegal immigrants, they are often paid very little and have no protection from unscrupulous employers.

In Miami, some Hispanics from Cuba and, more recently, from Colombia are reported as being involved in importing drugs and in other illegal activities. Laws have been introduced to try to improve the rights and living standards of African Americans and Hispanics but these have led to further problems.

Ideology - What is Capitalism?

Capitalism is an ideology, a set of beliefs, in which most Americans believe. Everyone is free to set up a business and make a profit from it. They can also own property and charge others rent for its use. Under this system, the government encourages individuals to look after their own affairs and will only get involved when it is necessary. They will therefore keep taxes low, encourage people to pay for their own health care and education and keep government involvement to a minimum. When people take advantage of these opportunities, it helps them to have a high standard of living.

Rights and responsibilities - What is the American Dream?

Under the 'American Dream', all citizens have the same rights and opportunities. All have the right to set up a business and work hard. If the business is successful, they also have a right to make profits. It also suggests that your gender, race or religion will not stop you from being a success. In the USA, there are a number of rights and freedoms which help Americans achieve the 'American Dream'.

US citizens give up some of their rights to their state governments and the Federal Government. The Constitution identifies the things that the States and the Federal Government can do. Anything not identified is the right of the citizen. Any attempt by government to do something that is not set down in the Constitution would be declared unconstitutional and would not be allowed by the courts. The Bill of Rights, which is part of the Constitution, identifies specific rights that each citizen has:

What rights do Americans have?

- freedom of speech;
- freedom to demonstrate;
- freedom of movement;
- the right to a free trial;
- the right to carry a gun for protection;
- the right to vote;
- the right to join a political party;
- the right to join an interest group (pressure group);
- the right to work for a political party or interest group;
- freedom of the press.

New York

How are the rights of American people protected by the Constitution?

Over 200 years ago, America produced a document called the Constitution. In this document, the rights and responsibilities of the government and the people are recorded. If any individual finds that their rights are violated, they can use the courts to make sure that it does not happen again, or get compensation from those who have deprived them of their rights.

Participation – How can Americans participate in politics?

The USA is a democratic country. In countries with this ideology, governments are elected by the people of the country. Different political parties are allowed to put forward their ideas and the electorate (the people allowed to vote) are able to choose the representatives and the party which they want to govern them. Elections must be held at regular and frequent intervals.

Freedom is important in a democracy. The American people are free to take part (participate) in politics in a number of ways, including voting in elections for representatives. Americans are given the chance to vote in many different elections including:

◆ Federal – Presidential, Senate, House of Representatives;
◆ State – Governor, Senate, House of Representatives;
◆ Local Levels – Dog Catcher, Sheriff, District Attorney, Judge.

Americans are also free to stand for election. Some join political parties and interest groups. As members, they will be involved in a number of activities that will help the group or party. This might include writing letters, phoning people, collecting money, lobbying representatives, demonstrating, producing posters, leaflets and TV broadcasts.

They can also contact their elected representative to ask for their help on particular issues. Gun control and abortion are very important issues for many Americans.

Ideology – The US system of government

Government in the USA is divided into:

◆ State Government;
◆ Federal Government.

State government

Each state in the USA has its own government which makes laws for the people of that state. There are fifty state governments in the US. This means that something which is legal in one state may be illegal in another. State governments have control over a number of issues including:

◆ education;
◆ housing;
◆ economic planning;
◆ roads;
◆ crime and punishment;
◆ the age people can marry;
◆ whether gambling is legal or not.

Capitol Building

Federal Government

The Federal Government controls national affairs and international affairs.

When a major (federal) crime is committed in one state and the criminals escape to another state, it is the Federal Bureau of Investigation (FBI) rather than the state police who pursue the criminals. Federal government is involved in funding education especially when states are not doing the job properly. State law and federal law may sometimes come into conflict. The Federal Government also controls the mail service and issues currency.

It is the sole right of the Federal Government to control USA relations with other countries. It controls treaties, the armed forces and sends ambassadors to foreign countries.

The Constitution

This is the set of rules which outlines:

1. What the Federal Government can and cannot do – its powers and jurisdiction.
2. The structure of the Federal Government – who can be candidates, dates of elections.
3. What each branch of government can and cannot do.

Branches of the Federal Government

There are three branches of government:

◆ The legislative branch - the people who make the law. This is called Congress and is made up of the House of Representatives and the Senate.
◆ The executive branch - the people who administer (carry out) the law. This is the President, his cabinet and his advisers.
◆ The judicial branch - the people who judge whether laws are constitutional (allowed by the Constitution). This is the Supreme Court. All appeals are decided by the Supreme Court.

The Separation of Powers

The different branches of government are kept separate to prevent any one person becoming too powerful.

The judicial branch can stop the President or the Congress changing laws to make themselves more powerful. Congress can block the President and the President can prevent the Congress doing things. The House of Representatives can stop the Senate and vice versa. This system is called checks and balances. The power of any one branch of government is held in check by the others and its power is balanced against their power.

The Congress

The Congress consists of the Senate and the House of Representatives

The Senate

◆ There are 100 Senators, two from each of the 50 states.
◆ Senators are elected for 6 years.

House of Representatives

◆ There are 435 Congressmen/women (members of the House of Representatives). Each Congressman/woman represents about 300,000 voters.
◆ Congressmen/women are elected for 2 years.
◆ The number of Congressmen/women from each state depends on the number of people who live in that state.

Political parties

There are two main political parties in the USA:

◆ The Democratic Party;
◆ The Republican Party.

Both parties believe in Capitalism and in the American Dream.

Ethnic minority participation

Few Hispanic Americans are successful politically because they don't have the money to pay for election campaigns and their experience from their country of origin means that they may not trust politicians.

Some African Americans find it hard to make political progress because some whites are unwilling to vote for an African American candidate. Some still hold racist views about people from a different ethnic background. Also, as so few African Americans have become representatives, many think it is a waste of time to stand for election. What is the point of standing when no one will vote for you? Even when they do get elected, there is not the budget to improve things in the inner city areas in which they often live.

In the 2000 election, 21 Hispanics and 39 African Americans were elected to the House of Representatives. There were no African Americans or Hispanic Americans elected to the Senate.

The White House

Results of the November 2004 Federal Elections

Presidential Election Results (2004)

	Popular Votes	Electoral Votes
George W. Bush	59,459,351 (51%)	286
John Kerry	55,950,097 (48%)	252
Ralph Nader	400,701	0

Senate Results (2004)

	Seats
Republicans	55
Democrats	44
Independent	1
Total	100

House of Representatives (2000)

	Seats
Republicans	234
Democrats	200
Independent	1
Total	435

Inequality – Why do some Americans have a higher standard of living than others?

Some Americans have a high standard of living because they work hard and run profitable businesses, while others have never had the same opportunities because they have never had access to a good education. They may also face discrimination and prejudice, which will stop them from getting jobs which they are qualified to do.

Those Americans who do go to good schools and colleges have a better chance of getting a good job than those who leave education at an early age or never gain proper qualifications.

According to the 'American Dream', all Americans have the chance to work hard and make their fortune. However, many people do work hard but are never given the chance to run or manage a business.

Inequality – Why are African Americans and Hispanic Americans less likely to achieve social, political and economic success in the USA?

The development of an African American middle class, i.e., African Americans moving into white collar and professional positions that were traditionally occupied by whites, shows that some progress has been made. However, many African Americans still live on or below the poverty line.

Although more African Americans have moved to the affluent suburbs, it is often to housing areas that are 'segregated'.

Many African Americans find it hard to be a success because they live in run-down, inner city housing estates. In these areas, the chance of getting a good job is poor and therefore many people find it difficult to meet their needs and wants. To escape from these conditions, they often turn to drugs and crime. This may result in them using all their money to feed a drug habit or finding it even harder to get a job because they have a criminal record.

◆ African American unemployment rates are higher;
◆ African Americans have fewer qualifications than whites;
◆ African Americans are less likely to attend college or university;
◆ African American infant mortality is much higher than that of whites;
◆ the majority of urban African Americans and Hispanics live in ghettos in the inner city;

Features of Ghetto Life

◆ *sub-standard housing;*
◆ *poor medical services;*
◆ *crime;*
◆ *murder is the major cause of death in the 15 to 34 age range for African American males;*
◆ *drug abuse;*
◆ *poverty;*
◆ *single parent families headed by women;*
◆ *unemployment;*
◆ *AIDS;*
◆ *Tuberculosis (TB).*

For young people living in these areas, there are very few positive role models. The successful people tend to be drug dealers, prostitutes or gang members. This means that many give up education at an early age because academic qualifications will not help them to survive in the inner city areas. Many African Americans also face discrimination because some people refuse to treat them as equals. This may mean that they find it hard to get jobs or get promoted. Some attempts have been made to reduce inequality.

Hispanic Americans also face many of the problems associated with living in the inner city areas. However, they also find it difficult to be a success because they have come from a Spanish speaking country such as Mexico. This means that they will find it hard to complete forms and find work. Some Hispanic Americans may also be illegal immigrants. To get work, they have to be willing to work in poor conditions and for low wages, otherwise the authorities may find out and send them back to their country of origin.

The Standard of Living of Some American Groups – Key Statistics

	White	African American	Hispanic American
Education (obtaining University degree)	23%	12%	10.0%
Percentage of group in poverty	10%	31%	25%
Infant mortality (death within first year of birth)	8%	17%	14%
Language	English	English	Spanish
Percentage of the population	75%	12.5%	9.8%
Life expectancy (males)	73	65	68

Affirmative Action

Affirmative action programmes tried to reduce inequalities in education and employment. One scheme was bussing.

Bussing

This was an attempt to integrate African Americans and whites in the schools. Previously, whites in a white area tended to go to an all white school whereas African Americans went to an all black school.

Bussing has caused many problems: violence in schools between pupils, violence in the streets from parents, demonstrations against the buses from both African Americans and whites who did not like their children going to school outside the local community.

Quotas

Places were reserved in college for people from poorer backgrounds so that they could get into college with fewer qualifications than their fellow students.

This led to ill feeling from whites who could not get into college while someone with fewer qualifications got a place. This quota system of reserved places was eventually declared unconstitutional because it was reverse discrimination.

Why do these political, social and economic inequalities continue to exist?

◆ Though the law prohibits discrimination in employment, housing and education, African Americans and Hispanics continue to suffer discrimination because the law cannot alter people's prejudices.
◆ Political progress is slow because most minorities think it is a waste of time for them to participate. Most minorities think that the political system has failed them socially and economically. Their 'dream of the promised land' (Martin Luther King, 1967) has been shattered.
◆ In the 1980s, Affirmative Action was diluted by President Reagan. It failed to help most African Americans.
◆ The economic problems faced by the USA in the latter part of the twentieth century harmed the poor a great deal more than the rich. Ethnic minorities are well-represented among the USA's poor.
◆ The circle of poverty continues to prevent African Americans from achieving a better lifestyle.

The Statue of Liberty

Russia

In 1985, Mikhail Gorbachev became the leader of the Soviet Union (USSR). Until then, the Soviet Union was a Communist country. Gorbachev introduced a number of changes. These eventually led to:

◆ the breakup of the USSR;
◆ the development of democracy;
◆ the introduction of Capitalism.

When the Soviet Union broke up, it split into fifteen separate countries, one of which was Russia. In terms of area, Russia is the largest country in the world, with about 150 million people. The Soviet Union used to be one of the world's superpowers but, after the change from Communism, Russia has found it hard to maintain this position.

Changing ideology

An ideology is a set of ideas or beliefs which determine how a country will be run. The Soviet Union had a Communist ideology. In theory, under Communism:

◆ there were no class divisions. Therefore, there was less inequality, no very rich or very poor people. Everyone was equal.
◆ all the factories, buildings, land and farms were owned by the government on behalf of the people.
◆ everyone was guaranteed the right to work and the right to free education and medical treatment.
◆ everyone was looked after in times of need, e.g., in old age.
◆ since the Communist party represented the people, there was no need for any other political party.

Moscow State University

Gorbachev introduced changes in three main areas.

Reforming the economy

'Perestroika' was the name given to the reform of the economy. Factories were encouraged to improve the quality of the goods they produced. They were also encouraged to manufacture as much as they could sell and keep any profit. Thus, industry had to become more modern and high-tech in order to compete in the market. Also, people were encouraged to set up their own private businesses and farms and keep any profits.

More freedoms

During the period known as 'glasnost' (openness), Gorbachev opened up life in the Soviet Union by encouraging people to express their views and opinions openly without fear of repression. The media was also allowed to put forward opinions other than the official government point of view.

More democracy

The country was made more democratic. Elections took place. The voters could choose from several political parties instead of just the Communist party.

The impact of the changes

These changes have had dramatic effects on the lives of people in Russia. The Russian economy is moving from Communism towards a Capitalist system. In theory, under Capitalism:

◆ people can set up their own businesses. They can make profits or losses. If they make big profits, other businesses will be encouraged to join in and there will be competition.
◆ the price of any good or service is fixed by the market, i.e., the relationship between supply (the number and quality of the good or service being produced) and demand (the amount of the good or service people want to buy).
◆ people have a choice of goods;
◆ the government interferes as little as possible in the economy.

The Russian political system has moved from Communism towards a democratic system of government.

◆ the government is elected by the people;
◆ there is a choice of political parties;
◆ freedom is important:

- *freedom of speech;*
- *freedom of choice;*
- *freedom to vote;*
- *freedom of the media;*
- *freedom from repression.*

Russia – the political system

A constitution was agreed in December 1993, which set up a new system of government. This included:

◆ a President;
◆ a Cabinet;
◆ a Federal Assembly made up of two houses.

The upper house is called the Federation Council. The lower house is called the Duma.

Power of the President

The Constitution gave a lot of power to the President. The President could:

◆ ignore the wishes of the Federal Assembly (the new legislature) and appoint a prime minister of his choice;
◆ veto laws passed by the Federal Assembly;
◆ dissolve the Federal Assembly.

In what ways have the social and political lives of Russian people changed in recent years?

Effects of economic change in Russia

The Russian economy moved from a state controlled command economy under Communism towards a Capitalist economy. This caused many problems for the Russian people as the economy changed its structure.

◆ unemployment;

◆ falling living standards;

◆ a rapidly rising crime rate. However, crime is low compared to most western countries;

◆ the old economy was geared towards arms production. Many food and consumer goods factories were very old fashioned.

CASE STUDY
Elections in Russia

Russia is a federal presidential democratic republic divided into 49 oblasts, 21 republics, 10 autonomius okrugs, 6 krays and 2 federal cities.

Executive
President: Vladimir Vladimirovic Putin (2000)
Chairman of the Government: Michail Fradkov (2004)
The president is elected for a four year term by the people.

Election of President: 14 March 2004 (64.3 % turnout)

Vladimir Vladimirovic Putin	71.2%
Nikolaj Michajlovic Charitonov	13.7%
Sergej Jurievic Glaz'ev	4.1%
Irina Mutsuovna Chakamada	3.9%
Oleg Aleksandrovic Malyckin	2.0 %
Sergej Michajlovic Mironov	0.8%

Source (adapted): www.rferl.org/Central Election Commission (TsIK)

Parliament
The Federal Assembly has two chambers. The State Duma has 450 members, elected for a four year term, 225 members elected in single-seat constuencies and 225 members by proportional representation. The Federation Council has 178 members: 2 delegates for each region.

Main Political Parties
These include the Agrarian Party of Russia, United Russia, Unity, Russian Democratic Party, Communist Party of the Russian Federation, Liberal Democratic Party of Russia, People's Party of the Russian Federation, Party of Russia's Rebirth, Motherland - National Patriottic Union, Russian Party of Life, Russian Pensioners' Party, Russian Party of Social Justice, Social Democratic Party of Russia, Union of Right Forces, Women of Russia.

Why do some Russians have a higher living standard than others?

Inequality in Russia has increased due to the economic changes which have taken place. After the fall of Communism, the gap between the rich and poor increased. Some groups have struggled to meet their basic needs. The 1993 Russian Constitution guaranteed certain rights to the people of Russia. It guaranteed citizens access to social security, pensions, free health care and 'affordable' housing but no longer guaranteed them a job. This means that they may find it hard to get enough money to meet the basic needs of their family. This is also made worse because the prices of goods in the shops has increased (inflation).

In the past, the government would have tried to help by giving benefits to those in need. However, it is no longer able to do so.

At the same time, many Russians have benefited from the changes. Some people have been able to set up businesses and have made large profits from them. This will give them a much higher standard of living than under the Communist system. Some people have become richer because:

- they can now set up their own private businesses and make their own profits. There is now a new breed of Russian 'biznesmeni' who have so much money that they can afford to buy cars and houses as status symbols. In addition, red brick two-storey houses with a garage, sauna and billiard room are being built around cities like Moscow.
- the government no longer controls wage levels. If workers work hard, they can earn more money. Russians are buying western goods such as chocolate bars, drink, cigarettes, electrical goods and shoes. As the standard of living of some Russians has increased, many shops and companies from Europe, the USA and the Far East have started to sell goods and provide services (including McDonalds, IBM and BP). This means that there is a greater variety of goods and services available.
- companies can compete with each other. This means that there is an incentive to produce good quality goods which people will buy.
- cooperatives have been set up where people pool their resources and then share in any profit which is made.

Some people have become poorer because:

- there is no longer a guaranteed right to a job and some people are unemployed. Official unemployment figures are low but many people are on unpaid leave or working reduced hours.
- under Capitalism, there are great inequalities. Some people get rich at the expense of others.
- prices have risen steeply and people cannot afford to buy the basic necessities. High inflation erodes wages and those people on fixed incomes suffer particular hardships.

- there are no universal welfare benefits as there were under Communism. This means that people are not always cared for in times of need, e.g., in old age or when unemployed.

In what ways have the Russian people been able to participate more fully?

One of the changes introduced means that people can participate more fully in running their country. Before 'glasnost', many people were denied the right to participate.

People who spoke out against life in the Soviet Union were called 'dissidents'. Many of these dissidents were watched closely by the KGB, put in prison, sent to labour camps, or sent into internal exile.

- Human rights dissidents.
  They wanted the right to speak freely, to criticise the government, to protest and to oppose the Communist party.
- Religious dissidents.
  Religion was not banned in the Soviet Union. However, the government made it difficult for people to follow their own religion.
- Nationalist dissidents.
  These people wanted independence for the republics that made up the Soviet Union. They were harshly treated by the government.

Since glasnost, people can now participate in the following ways:

- nearly all dissidents have been released;
- the media encourages people to put forward their own views about life in Russia;
- there is now a choice of political parties;
- there is a choice of candidates;
- people have been allowed to protest and demonstrate against the government;
- the secret police is no longer as powerful;
- people have the right to join a pressure group;
- there is a new constitution with increased rights.

Have rights and freedoms improved since Communism ended?

Generally speaking, Russians have more rights today than under the old Communist system. They are able to start political parties and encourage others to join. This will give them more freedom to express their opinions. If they are very unhappy, they can demonstrate or protest to highlight a problem and make more people aware of it. This has been the case recently with demonstrations about the mafia and the low level of benefits for the elderly.

They can also highlight problems on TV and in newspapers. In the past, these were controlled by the Communist party. They have much more freedom to criticise the government. However, not everyone agrees.

Chechnya – A Case Study

The Place
Chechnya is a small mountainous area of central Russia.

The People
The Chechen people are mainly Muslim. Although the Chechens have different cultural and religious beliefs to the Russian people, they continue to be ruled by the Russian government to which they are opposed.

The History
When the Soviet Union collapsed in 1991, a number of republics broke away from Russia and became independent, for example, Latvia, Belarus and Georgia. However, Chechnya's request to be independent was turned down by Russian President Boris Yeltsin in order to prevent the break-up of the Russian Federation. Some would argue that this decision was also about protecting Russia's important oil pipelines in the region.

Increasing tension between the Russian government and Chechnya developed into open warfare in 1994. It is claimed that more than 80,000 civilians have died over the last ten years. The Russian army was forced to withdraw in 1996, although Chechnya still remained part of the Russian Federation.

A number of groups have emerged willing to use terrorist methods to continue the fight for independence. In 2000, Russian President Vladimir Putin attempted to use force to defeat these groups. Russian troops were accused of human rights violations including looting, burning homes and buildings and executions.

Some of these Chechen terrorist groups have been linked to Al Qaeda and the killing of more than 340 people at the Beslan School in September 2004.

Those who support the view that rights and freedoms have improved argue:

◆ glasnost has meant that people can now freely express their views without fear of repression;
◆ there is increased media freedom;
◆ people can travel abroad;
◆ people can follow whatever religion they wish;
◆ dissidents are no longer persecuted;
◆ the KGB has been reformed;
◆ the people now have a choice of political parties and candidates;
◆ there is now economic freedom. People can choose to set up their own businesses if they wish. Factory managers now have more freedom to decide on what goods to produce.

Those who oppose the view that rights and freedoms have improved state:

◆ there is still violence and fighting in many of the republics. These are accompanied by human rights abuse;
◆ there are restrictions on the media;
◆ with the downfall of Communism, many rights are now being denied, e.g., the right to a job, the right to benefits for all;
◆ many people are suffering economically. They are unemployed and cannot afford to buy even the basic necessities;
◆ the health service is collapsing;
◆ there is a rapid increase in crime in Russia. Many rich businessmen are members of the various 'mafia-style' criminal organisations that control the economy in many parts of the country;
◆ there has been a rise in extremist political parties especially neo-fascist groups who would deny Russians some of their existing rights;
◆ the Russian Constitution does not give the Parliament, which represents the wishes of the people, very many powers.

With all the political changes comes a number of social problems. In the past, the Communist government looked after everyone and all Russians were promised work. This is no longer the case and a lot of people have found themselves living in poverty. The new government cannot afford to pay out benefits to the same extent. Sometimes the only opportunity is to turn to crime. This has resulted in an increase in prostitution, drugs and mafia violence.

Why do some members of national groups within Russia feel they are not treated fairly?

◆ People who live in rural areas feel that they are disadvantaged compared to people living in urban areas. Services such as education and health are much better in the cities and towns and life is often more primitive in the countryside.
◆ Many national groups are uncertain of foreign workers and migrants. They are worried that these 'foreigners' will take the jobs from the people that live there and will not pay taxes to the government.
◆ Many national groups would like to run their own affairs and feel that they are not given the right to make decisions that will affect them.

In what ways does the Russian government now encourage foreign business to open in places such as Moscow?

◆ If new businesses open, it may make the government more popular because it will increase the number of goods available in the shops and also help to improve the standard of living of the people.
◆ It will earn Russia valuable foreign currency, which can be used to purchase goods abroad.
◆ As the standard of living and the number of good quality shops increases, more tourists will be attracted to the country. This will increase the demand for goods and services and again bring valuable foreign currency into the country.

With the increase in tourists and foreign businesses, more employment opportunities will become available. This will help to cut unemployment. It will also improve conditions for the workers and bring improvements in pay.

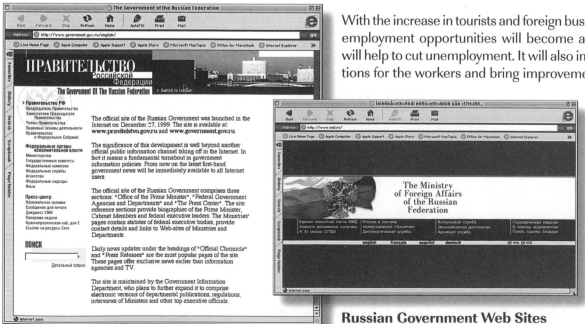

Russian Government Web Sites

China

China has the largest population of any country in the world (1,232,083,000). Most people (72%) work in agriculture. There are 56 officially recognised nationalities. The Head of State is Jiang Zemin and Hu Jintao is the Vice-President.

Ideology – Communism

An ideology is a set of ideas or beliefs which determine how a country will be run. China has a Communist ideology. Communism is a set of economic and political theories (ideas). In theory, Communism means that:

◆ everyone is equal;
◆ all factories, businesses and agriculture are owned by the state (government) on behalf of the people;
◆ the economy is planned by the government;
◆ the government will control prices and the supply of goods and services;
◆ everyone will receive roughly the same amount of pay because everyone is important;
◆ everyone should have:
  • *free education;*
  • *free medical care;*
  • *housing;*
  • *a job;*
  • *the right to be cared for in old age.*

◆ The Communist party represents the people so there is no need for more than one political party.

The Chinese Communist party

The Communist party runs all levels of government from the committees which organise the villages, farms and factories to national level. Only about 4% of the Chinese people are members of the Communist party (52 million members). 30 million of these are cadres – full time party officials or managers of the state-owned firms. The party's most powerful group is the seven member standing committee of the Politiburo. The Politiburo decides the main policies of China. At local level, local Communist party officials explain government policy. Committees are formed to implement this policy.

The Chinese Communist party does not allow opposition to its rule because:

◆ China is a one party state. "The party knows best";
◆ the Communist ideology does not allow dissent. Dissent means that something is wrong and Communist ideology cannot be wrong. Therefore, dissent cannot exist and is not tolerated. The 1989 Tiananmen Square protest was not tolerated by the Communist party. It ordered the People's Liberation Army to crush the dissent.

In what ways have the recent economic reforms given Chinese people many new rights and responsibilities?

◆ the 'four modernisations' have encouraged individuals to set up their own businesses;
◆ some firms are making large profits;
◆ extra rights for workers working in the 'special economic zones and super trade zones'.

How have the human rights of the Chinese people changed in recent years?

Although there are few political freedoms in China, economic rights have improved. People are free to make a profit in certain areas and there is more contact with foreign businesses and markets.

It is also possible to have more say in local politics (neighbourhood committees). However, other candidates cannot stand against the Communist party in elections.

Equality – Why do some Chinese people have higher living standards than others?

In theory, all Chinese people are equal. Some parts of China have developed more than others in recent years. This gives people living in these areas the chance of a much higher standard of living. However, many people living in rural areas still struggle to meet their needs. Hong Kong is a good example of an area with a good standard of living. You are also more likely to be wealthy if you live in a town or city rather than in the countryside.

Many foreign companies want to set up in China because they see it as one of the biggest and fastest growing markets in the world. If you are employed by such a firm, you are likely to get a higher income than someone working for a Chinese firm.

Finally, if you are a member of the Communist party, you will have a higher standard of living than a non-member, because you will have access to privileges such as good housing and health care.

Equality – rural areas

- many rural areas are very poor:
  In Gansu province:
  - *34% of the 18.9 million peasants live below the poverty line;*
  - *59 of the 86 counties in Gansu rely on government aid to keep the people from dying of starvation;*
  - *many families (90%) have no household water supply;*
  - *33% of the region has no electricity.*

- Deng Xiaoping's 'responsibility system' abolished Mao's collective farms and restored households as the unit of production. Crops could now be sold on the free market. All the land used to be owned by the state and farmers had to grow certain crops ordered by the state. All crops were given to the state. Now farmers can farm on a private basis but still have to provide grain to feed the people in the cities. Once they have provided their share, they can sell the rest for profit for themselves. Therefore, people can now set up their own private businesses and keep the profit. This is called the 'responsibility system'.

However, all is not well. The government has not managed to pay the farmers for their crops. Many farmers cannot 'seek medical attention, pay for their children's education or buy daily necessities because they cannot get the money they have earned'. IOUs have been given to the farmers.

Equality between rural and urban areas

- Millions of Chinese are moving from rural areas to the towns and cities like Beijing and Shanghai. It is estimated that, by the year 2020, the number of people living in cities will double from 350 million to 700 million. They are being forced off the land by poor incomes and increased mechanisation. They are attracted to the cities by higher wages and better living conditions.

A Chinese market

© Owen Franken/Corbis

Equality in urban areas

◆ Many Chinese people no longer work for the state. 'Township and village enterprises' (TVES) are light industrial groups with shared ownership. These employ 90 million people. They account for more than one third of China's industrial output;

◆ Areas/cities such as Guangdong and Shenzhen have 'special economic zone' status. These are growth areas. Industry and especially foreign investment are attracted to these areas. However, there are also problems such as corruption, especially within the Communist party;

◆ Life for workers in the state-owned and privately-owned factories is not too good:

- *working conditions are appalling. In the first 10 months of 1993, there were 65,000 deaths in industrial accidents;*

- *state-owned factories cannot compete with foreign imports. Workers in these factories have been told to stay at home. They receive no salary and no benefits. The workers are becoming restless and the government is worried. It has arrested a number of leading trade union officials because they have been asking for the right to strike and for the legalisation of independent workers' unions;*

- *in the special economic zones, workers get their wages but the working conditions are very poor. For example, in November 1993, 84 workers at a factory in Shenzen were killed in a fire when they were locked in to make sure they met orders.*

◆ Many Communist party members now own businesses and hope to become rich. However, this goes against Communist ideology. Beijing is going 'consumer mad'. A few years ago, a refrigerator was a big status symbol. Now everyone has one. Colour televisions, washing machines and fridges are common. One family in five in Shanghai owns shares in a business.

In what ways does the government limit the political rights of Chinese citizens?

◆ waged political campaigns against those suspected of opposing the government;

◆ appealed to nationalism, state security and social stability for support for its policies;

◆ cracked down on ethnic and religious minorities in outlying regions;

◆ used the ¯strike hard~ campaign against crime. This resulted in the death penalty and harsh prison sentences, often without due process, as well as the use of torture and ill-treatment to obtain confessions from criminal suspects.

Source: Amnesty International Report 2003

Chinese People's Liberation Army

Participation

How can people participate in the economic life of China?

People can participate in the economic life of China in the following ways:

- specialised households are small scale private enterprise units which produce a limited range of goods or services, e.g., fish farms;
- people can now own their own land. This gives them the freedom to choose what and how much they produce;
- farmers can make additional money by selling the extra produce that they grow;
- in areas with special economic status, there is competition between businesses. Firms can choose what goods to produce and at what price to sell them;
- workers can be paid bonuses. They can choose whether to work extra hours or not.

Restrictions to economic participation

- economic reforms have not been introduced to all parts of China;
- only those with good land have benefited from the agricultural reforms;
- capital (money) is needed to start off a specialised household;
- a minority is getting rich at the expense of the majority.

In what ways does the Chinese government now encourage foreign business to open in China?

- If a new business opens, it may make the government more popular because the number of goods available in the shops will increase and the people's standard of living will improve
- It will earn China valuable foreign currency, which can be used to purchase other goods from abroad.
- As the standard of living and the number of good quality shops increases, more and more tourists will be attracted to the country. This will increase the demand for goods and services and again bring valuable foreign currency into the country.

With the increase in tourists and foreign business, more employment opportunities will become available. This will help to cut unemployment. It will also improve conditions for workers and bring increases in wages.

How can people participate in politics in China?

Many people believe that the Chinese people cannot participate in politics. This is not the case. They can take part by joining neighbourhood committees and workplace decision-making groups. These organisations will give people the chance to have their say in matters which will affect them. They can join and work for the Communist party. This will give them some more influence. However, if they don't agree with the Communist party, they are free to attend meetings organised by other groups although these groups are not allowed to stand against the Communist party in elections. They also have the chance to vote in elections. Although all the candidates are from the Communist party, there is a choice of candidate.

People can participate in the political life of China by:

- joining the Communist party;
- electing officials put forward by the Communist party;
- participating at village and local levels by electing officials through neighbourhood units. In neighbourhood units, everyone takes part in discussions and voting.
- Voting which takes place every 3 years;
- Voting for candidates for the Local People's Congress who then send delegates to the National People's Congress;
- Participating in other political groups including those expressing dissent.

Political Parties in China	
Party	**Membership**
Communist Party	57,000,000
China Democratic League	105,000
China Democratic National Construction Associates	50,000
China Association for Promoting Democracy	40,000
China Revolutionary Committee of the Kuomintang	40,000
China Peasants and Workers Democratic Party	40,000
Sisvan Society	40,000
Chinese Party for the Public Interest	10,000

Restrictions to political participation

- the 'four big rights' (see page 45) were withdrawn after Tiananmen Square;
- there are restrictions on human rights;
- there is control and repression at town/local level;
- China is a one party state;
- China operates a 'one child' policy.

What are the arguments used by Chinese people who want more political rights?

◆ Many Chinese people would agree that they need more political rights because they do not have the basic political rights that most other people around the world enjoy.

◆ Many Chinese people are also concerned that the legal system is not fair. They are concerned that individuals can be found guilty of crimes they are not responsible for. They are also worried that the Communist Party has too much influence over judges and that this results in the harsh treatment of citizens who have been critical of the government.

◆ Although there has been an increase in elections at local level, this has not been the case at the national level. This means that people in China do not have the opportunity to exert influence at national level or to change the government if it is not doing a good job. This means that there is no real democracy in China.

◆ The people of China do not have a right to free speech. If they speak out against the government, they may find themselves arrested or put in prison. If China is going to become a democracy, all citizens should be able to voice their opinions to a government which listens.

Rights and responsibilities

The Chinese Communist party has restricted human rights in China. The 'four big rights' were removed from the Constitution in 1980. These were the right to:

◆ speak out freely;
◆ air views freely;
◆ hold great debates;
◆ write big character posters.

What actions does the government take against people who speak out?

◆ execute by shooting;
◆ torture;
◆ imprisonment;
◆ public trial;
◆ detention without trial (anyone who sets up an unofficial organisation can be detained for 15 days);
◆ house arrest;
◆ police terror, beatings, arbitrary confinement and petty harassment.

What other limitations to freedom are there?

Media

◆ visitors arriving in China are supposed to hand in any foreign newspapers they may be carrying;
◆ satellite television worries the Chinese leadership. The events in Tiananmen Square were shown on satellite television both inside China and to the rest of the world. The government has now banned satellite TV from hotels and in Chinese homes. Shops are not allowed to sell satellite dishes;
◆ telephones and the internet also worry the Chinese leadership. Chinese dissidents use the internet to keep in touch with human rights groups abroad. Telephones also make it difficult for the government to control the flow of information.

Neighbourhood Units

The main functions of a neighbourhood unit

◆ to enforce the government's 'one child' policy;
◆ to keep an eye on the teenagers. They are not allowed to have friends of the opposite sex. This helps the 'one child' policy;
◆ to make sure that people in the neighbourhood have permission to be there. This cuts down on crime;
◆ to make sure that no one breaks the law;
◆ to keep the neighbourhood tidy;
◆ to make sure elderly people are looked after.

Arguments for neighbourhood units

✓ people can participate in the running of their community;
✓ people are concerned about others and not just themselves;
✓ the elderly are cared for;
✓ crime is kept down;
✓ government policy is followed.

Arguments against neighbourhood units

✗ personal freedom is restricted;
✗ although it appears to be a means of participation, it is, in fact, a means of control. The government tells the people what to do, e.g., for what and for whom to vote. It is often difficult for people to participate fully both economically and politically.

Family life

China has the largest population in the world. Its population is growing very quickly. Several ways are being tried to reduce population growth. These government policies are seen as a violation of human rights.

◆ the legal age for marrying has been raised from 20 to 22 for men and 18 to 20 for women. The 'recommended' ages, however, are 28 for men and 25 for women;

◆ family planning – the Chinese constitution says that it 'advocates and encourages family planning'. Birth control pills and other methods of contraception are delivered free to people's homes. Family planning centres are set up in neighbourhood units and 'family planning motivators' go to rural and urban areas to teach birth control;

◆ 'One is enough' – the one child policy. The government encourages families to have only one child. Couples with one child receive benefits:
  * *monthly bonus;*
  * *preference for housing;*
  * *better education for the child.*

These benefits are withdrawn if a second child is born. If a third child is born then wages are reduced by 5-10%.

Other effects of this policy:

◆ in many parts of China, the pressure to have a son is so strong that many baby girls disappear soon after birth (killed or abandoned);

◆ peasants may be fined a year's wages;

◆ there have been some reports that pregnant women have been dragged from their homes to have abortions;

◆ there is now a shortage of young women to marry in some rural areas. Women are being kidnapped and sold as brides (people caught are executed!). Poorer men have difficulty finding wives while those with money can afford to buy a wife.

Chinese labour camps

To maintain its rule, the Chinese government has a forced labour camp system – Chinese laogai. Since 1949, 50 million men and women have been sent to laogai camps. Prisoners are brainwashed and 'reformed' through slave labour. They are threatened with torture and fear. They must renounce their beliefs and study Communism. Today, in China, there are about 1000 forced labour camps and about 10 million forced labourers. Many of the Tiananmen Square protesters are in these camps. Laogai enterprises produce half the country's rubber products, coal for the UK and tea for Japan. Also, the Chinese government carries out more executions in one year than all other countries put together.

Executions by Country (2003)	
China	726
Iran	108
Congo	102
USA	65
Vietnam	64
Saudi Arabia	53
Egypt	52
Singapore	19

Protestors in Tiananmen Square

© Peter Turnley/Corbis

Tiananmen Square

◆ 17 April 1989: Students call for democracy and reforms. Up to 100,000 demonstrate peacefully in Tiananmen Square in Beijing despite official warnings.

◆ 26 April 1989: People's Daily newspaper publishes Communist party attack on the protesters. Students are angry.

◆ 13 May 1989: 1000 students (later 3000) begin a hunger strike for democracy in Tiananmen Square. Televised appeal to end protest because of visit to China of Mr Gorbachev.

◆ 15 May 1989: Mr Gorbachev arrives at Beijing airport. Protest continues in Tiananmen Square.

◆ 16 May 1989: Deng Xiaoping and Mr Gorbachev meet to agree on China/Soviet relationships. 250,000 protest in Tiananmen Square. Appeals to end the demonstration are broadcast by the government on loudspeakers in the square.

◆ 17 May 1989: 1 million people now in Beijing to protest.

◆ 19 May 1989: Troops move into Beijing. State of emergency declared.

◆ 4 June 1989: Soldiers open fire with machine guns, flame throwers and tanks on thousands of unarmed protesters. Many hundreds killed.

Subsequent to the Tiananmen Square events, the Chinese government tried to control media reporting inside China. It also issued official statements to the foreign press. Citizens were not allowed to talk to foreign journalists. Hospitals were not allowed to give out information about casualties. Party officials encouraged people to inform on friends and relatives. Large rewards were offered to anyone who informed on or turned in any of the protesters. Confessions were extracted after torture. The government made up a 'wanted' list of protesters whom they wished to arrest. Many of these people went into hiding in China and abroad. The ones who were arrested have been executed or sent to the labour camps.

International Relations

What the SQA says may be tested in the examination.

Alliances

The reasons for countries joining and maintaining membership of organisations and alliances (European Union, NATO and the United Nations) – military, diplomatic and economic cooperation and conflict.

The ways in which the security interests of European countries are promoted through individual and collective measures.

Aid

◇ The politics of aid – why states and how the UN and its agencies meet the needs of developing countries in Africa.

Some questions on this topic which are typical of those asked in the exam.

Alliances

◇ Explain the arguments for and against expanding the membership of the European Union. (C)

◇ Describe ways in which a country can benefit from being a member of the European Union. (G)

Describe the advantages to countries of becoming members of the NATO Alliance. (G)

◆ Describe the economic and military actions which international organisations can take to bring peace to areas of conflict. (G)

Describe ways in which the European Union helps to meet the needs of its members. (G)

Describe the kinds of action which organisations such as NATO, the United Nations and the European Union can take in order to try to stop wars. (C/G)

◆ Describe ways in which membership of organisations such as the European Union and NATO helps European countries to meet their economic and military needs. (C)

◆ Why do some countries from the former Eastern Europe feel that their needs would be met by joining NATO? (G/C)

◆ Explain the economic benefits gained by countries which join the European Union. (C)

◆ Explain how alliances such as NATO can help to protect member countries from threats such as international terrorism. (C)

Aid

> ⚠ **Remember**
>
> **Questions in this section usually ask for examples from countries which you have studied.**

◆ Describe aid projects which would help to meet the needs of the poorest people in Africa. (G/C)

◆ Describe ways in which aid can meet the needs of African countries you have studied. (G)

◆ Describe how the agencies of the United Nations try to meet the needs of countries in Africa. (G/C)

◆ Describe ways in which countries in Europe can benefit from providing aid to countries in Africa. (G/C)

◆ Explain the social, economic and political factors which developed countries such as the UK take into account when deciding which African countries should receive aid. (C)

◆ Give reasons why civil war or debt has prevented many African countries from meeting the needs of their people. (C)

◆ Explain why aid given to African countries may not always reach those who need it most? (G/C)

◆ Describe the ways in which European countries provide aid to countries in Africa. (G)

Need

All states have needs to satisfy. Sometimes these needs are expressed in terms of the national interest. Often states cooperate with one another to meet those needs. You may be asked about meeting the needs of the developing world (Africa) and the work of the UN, EU and NATO.

Power

Relates to ways in which different countries try to meet their own interests and sometimes have to compete against others. You may need to look at military force, diplomatic persuasion, aid, sanctions and the law.

Alliances – Power and Need

How is power measured?

Some countries are able to protect their national interests better than others. This depends on how powerful the country is. A powerful country is one which has the economic and military power (strength) to look after its own interests when these are challenged by another country. Power depends on the following:

- **Size** – larger countries will have their own food and raw materials and will not depend so much on other countries. The most powerful countries will also have larger populations.

- **Wealth** – Gross National Product (GNP) is the measurement of all the things that are produced in a country in a certain period of time.
      The higher the GNP, the wealthier the country and the more power or influence it will have over other countries. Less wealthy countries may be influenced by the wishes of wealthier countries.

- **Military strength** – the size of the armed forces and number and types of weapons a country has will give it power and influence over other countries.

How can a country use its power?

- **Diplomatic power**
  A country may use its friendship with another country to protect and promote its own interests. The UK will make treaties with other countries to defend one another in case of attack. It will make treaties and sign agreements with other countries to improve trade.

- **Economic power**
  A country may use its wealth to enter into agreement with another country so it can protect and promote its own economic interests. A powerful developed country will use its economic power to influence poorer developing countries to try get their raw materials as cheaply as possible.

- **Military power**
  A country may use its military power to protect and promote its own defence interests. Several powerful countries, including the USA and the UK, invaded Iraq in 2003 because Saddam Hussein's weapons of mass destruction were a major threat. Tony Blair also stated that it was necessary to remove this "cruel and sadistic dictator" who was responsible for the murder of one million people.

Countries form alliances with other countries for various reasons:

- **Military/Defence**
  Countries may join together to meet the threat of attack from powerful neighbouring countries. The North Atlantic Treaty Organisation (NATO) is an example of this type of alliance. Sometimes countries join a coalition – this is a loose form of alliance which is not as binding on its members as an alliance. A coalition was formed to overthrow Saddam Hussein in 2003. Countries can leave a coalition more easily than they can leave an alliance.

- **Economics**
  Countries sometimes feel that their economies will benefit from being part of a trading arrangement with other countries. The European Union (EU) is an example of this.

- **Historical ties**
  The Commonwealth is based on countries which were previously part of the British Empire. Although nations such as Canada and Australia are robust democracies in their own right and although their populations are no longer predominantly British in origin, they still maintain membership of the Commonwealth.

- **Ethnic/culture**
  The Arab League is a group of Middle Eastern nations whose mutual interests derive from their Arab background and from their opposition to Israel.

- **To exercise market power**
  The Oil Producing and Exporting Countries (OPEC) have control of a huge proportion of the world's oil supplies. They meet regularly to decide production levels and, therefore, the price of oil.

- **To prevent war and to maintain peace**
  The United Nations was formed after World War II to try to maintain the peace. It has developed a great number of specialised agencies which involve themselves in tackling illiteracy, health, hunger and other humanitarian issues.

- **Political and economic stability**
  The success of the EU has made any further wars between France and Germany very unlikely.

The needs of countries

Countries, like people, have basic needs.

What does a country need?

- good trade links;
- good defence;

- jobs, food;
- fair government;
- money.

On their own, many countries could not adequately provide for themselves.

Often the needs of states can only be met by cooperating with other countries. For example, countries cooperate or trade with each other to obtain the food they need.

There are two other types of need that are met by cooperation:

- defence needs;
- economic needs.

Military alliances

How can the defence needs of a country be met by joining a military alliance?

One of the main needs of a country is strong defence. Even if it is not a very powerful country, it may still need to protect itself from other countries which are more powerful. To meet this need, countries cooperate with each other to form military alliances.

An alliance is when a group of countries cooperate with each other. When all countries in an alliance get together, they are very powerful and other countries may be deterred from attacking them.

Britain needs a strong defence. It needs to protect itself from other more powerful countries. To meet this need, Britain cooperated with other countries to form a military alliance called the North Atlantic Treaty Organisation (NATO).

⚠ Note

Alliances change over time. Countries can be members of more than one alliance at the same time. The European Union includes member countries from both NATO and the former Warsaw Pact. Members of alliances can fall out with each other – there were arguments within both NATO and the European Union over involvement in the war in Iraq.

North Atlantic Treaty Organisation

Members of NATO (2004)
USA, Canada, UK, France, Belgium, Netherlands, Luxembourg, Spain, Italy, Germany, Denmark, Iceland, Norway, Portugal, Greece, Turkey, Czech Republic, Hungary, Poland, Estonia, Lithuania, Latvia, Slovenia, Slovakia, Romania, Bulgaria.

Why was NATO needed?

At the end of the second world war, the USA, Britain and France feared that the USSR would try to turn the countries of Europe into Communist countries.

The USSR was a Communist country while the USA was a Capitalist country.

The USA and countries in Western Europe were afraid of being attacked by the USSR. Thus, in order to provide for their defence needs, they decided to cooperate and formed an alliance called the North Atlantic Treaty Organisation.

The aims of NATO

- to preserve peace and freedom;
- to prevent war;
- to establish a lasting peace in Europe;
- to protect western Europe from the USSR.

Warsaw Pact

Why was the Warsaw Pact needed?

The Warsaw Pact was set up in 1955 because the USSR did not trust the USA and the countries of Western Europe. The West opposes Communism and did not want Communism to spread. The USSR was protecting its needs by making sure that all the countries in Eastern Europe were on its side. It formed a military alliance for its own protection.

Members of the Warsaw Pact (in 1955)	
USSR	Hungary
Poland	Romania
East Germany	Bulgaria
Czechoslovakia	Albania

The Cold War

The Cold War was a period of tension between the USA and the USSR and their respective allies. The two sides became involved in a competition to prove that each was better than the other. The competition involved:

- the Arms Race – building up stocks of weapons;
- the Space Race;
- giving aid to other countries to ensure their support;
- giving out false information to the media;
- trying to achieve success in sports competitions.

The Arms Race

Each side tried to become more powerful than the other by building up more and more powerful and sophisticated weapons. It involved nuclear weapons of different types:

- strategic – long range weapons;
- theatre – medium range weapons;
- tactical – short range and conventional weapons like aircraft, tanks and ships.

The aim was to have so many weapons that it deterred the other side from attacking. However, the fear was that the other side was secretly building or developing more weapons. Thus, both sides continued to develop and build weapons until they reached the point where they could destroy the world thirty times over. This was called overkill.

Arms control

Both sides realised they had to slow down and stop the race. It was too costly and too dangerous. They slowly began to cooperate with each other through arms control agreements. This process was halted by the collapse of the Soviet Union and the Warsaw Pact.

The end of the Cold War

There are many reasons why the Cold War has ended.

Events in the USSR

The new era of cooperation in Europe was partly due to Mikhail Gorbachev becoming leader of the Soviet Union (USSR). The USSR faced economic, political and social problems which Gorbachev tried to solve through 'perestroika' and 'glasnost' (see page 36).

His policies failed and the Communist party lost control of events in the USSR and Eastern Europe.

The USSR split up into fifteen independent states which continued to cooperate in the Commonwealth of Independent States (CIS). Russia was the largest and most powerful country in the group. These changes affected other countries in Eastern Europe.

Events in Eastern Europe

- Poland – the Eastern Bloc's first non-Communist government.
- Hungary – Western experts were brought in to show how democracy should be organised. Presently, they have a political system with more than one political party.
- East Germany – in 1989, the Berlin Wall came down. Free elections were held in 1990. In 1992, East Germany and West Germany united to form one country.
- Czechoslovakia – free elections were held in 1990. Soon the country split in two – the Czech Republic and Slovakia.
- Romania – the leader of Romania was a dictator and would not give up power. Free elections were held in 1990 following a revolution.

Warsaw Pact collapses

The countries of Eastern Europe turned away from Communism and the control of the USSR. The Warsaw Pact collapsed. It no longer poses a threat to Western Europe.

Should NATO be kept?

Arguments for keeping NATO

✓ Communism has ended in Eastern Europe. However, it could start up again.

✓ NATO has helped keep the peace in Europe since 1945. It has worked well. Why get rid of it?

✓ Who knows when another war will break out? NATO might be needed to keep the peace in the future.

✓ Europe is more dangerous than ever. More countries are undergoing change that could involve disputes and war, e.g., the former Yugoslavia.

✓ When the USSR split, several of the new states got a share of the nuclear weapons. Europe is now a more dangerous place because of this proliferation of states with nuclear weapons.

Arguments against keeping NATO

✗ NATO was set up to protect Western European countries from the USSR and Communism. This threat no longer exists. The Warsaw Pact no longer exists. There is no need for NATO.

✗ European countries should form their own military alliance. They should not rely on help from the USA.

A changing role for NATO

NATO could be allowed to act as peacekeepers in European or world trouble spots such as Bosnia.

Its membership could be expanded to safeguard Europe's defence needs.

NATO may be called upon to help fight the 'War on Terrorism', which both President Bush and Prime Minister Blair regard as critically important. Not every member of NATO would, however, agree to the use of a defensive alliance in this way.

How alliances can work

Greece and Turkey have been in serious disagreement with each other for many years. They disagree about Cyprus and they disagree about boundaries in the Aegean Sea. Both are members of the United Nations and of NATO, while Turkey is bidding to join Greece in the European Union. They have come close to war on occasion. However, each time war has threatened, a solution has been found through their membership of these alliances.

- Alliances and groupings are changing all the time. New members join existing organisations. New alliances are formed.
- Some groups e.g. the UN and the EU – are very longstanding and stable; others – for example the coalition recently pulled together to deal with the situations in Afghanistan and Iraq – can be much looser and more temporary.
- Some countries are in several alliances. This can lead to difficulties if a policy of one clashes with a policy of another.
- The aims of alliances and international organisations can change over time. The European Union now involves itself in a much wider range of issues than it did when it was mainly concerned with trade among member countries.
- International groups sometimes join together. The United Nations, the Organisation for Security and Cooperation in Europe and the European Union have joined together to help the situation in Kosovo. Countries can also work with internationally recognised organisations such as the Red Cross.

The United Nations (UN)

The UN has now been in existence for over 50 years. Established in 1945 by 51 countries, there are now 189 members. It is a worldwide organisation and has a wide range of economic, social and political structures. When countries join the UN, they do not give up the power of making their own decisions. When states become members of the UN, they agree to accept the UN Charter and to support the four aims of the UN:

- to maintain international peace and security;
- to develop friendly relations among members;
- to cooperate in solving international problems;
- to act together to solve problems.

How is the UN organised?

- The General Assembly consists of representatives from each member country. This body is not elected and tends to deal with long term issues rather than immediate crises.
- The Security Council is a group of fifteen member countries which can be called into session very quickly at the request of a member of the UN. Five members – the UK, France, the USA, Russia and China, the 'permanent members' – are always on the Security Council. Each permanent member has a veto which allows it, on its own, to block any action proposed by the Security Council. Security Council decisions must have unanimous approval of the permanent members.

- The Economic and Social Council.
- The Trusteeship Council.
- The International Court of Justice.
- The Secretariat is the 'office staff' of the UN and is responsible for putting decisions into effect. It is not elected. The head of the Secretariat, the Secretary-General, often operates as a 'troubleshooter', trying to bring warring sides together or visiting areas where natural disasters like flood or famine have occurred.

In January 2005, Secretary-General Kofi Annan appealed for an unprecedented, global relief effort to assist countries affected by the tsunami which hit Indonesia, the Maldives, Sri Lanka, the Seychelles and Somalia on 26 December, 2004.

Achievements of the UN

Although much of the work of the UN is done outside Europe, its work is still important to European countries. For humanitarian reasons alone, better-off nations would want to help developing countries but there are also the advantages to be gained from trade.

Developing countries are often the source of the raw materials, food and manufactured goods which help to maintain, for instance, our standard of living. Again, as their economies develop, they are potential markets for products made in Europe. This brings profits to European companies.

Keeping the peace

This is a crucial aspect of the work of the UN. In the 1990s, the UN acted to restore democracy to Kuwait in the Gulf War and played a role in ending civil wars in Cambodia, Guatemala, El Salvador and Mozambique. Diplomacy is the approach the UN prefers to use although economic sanctions are sometimes imposed.

United Nations peacekeeping troops have continued to work in the Democratic Republic of the Congo (DRC). Their work, according to Kofi Annan in early 2005, is being hampered by human rights violations.

Disarmament

The UN tries to halt the spread of arms and attempts to eliminate the use of weapons of mass destruction. For example: in 1992, there was a treaty prohibiting the production/use of chemical weapons; in 1997, the Ottawa Convention outlawed landmines. This was signed by 100 countries.

Building the peace

The UN advises on, and supports, the maintenance of law and order. To help to establish stability within states, the UN supervises elections, runs a human rights office in Cambodia and has cleared mines in Mozambique.

However, success is not always guaranteed. In early

2005, the senior United Nations envoy for Sudan voiced concern that local authorities in the country's war-torn region of Darfur were harassing staff who worked for non-governmental organizations (NGOs).

Keeping the peace and working for peace

The UN Security Council sets up peacekeeping operations. The UN has been in Cyprus since 1964.

There are currently 35,400 military and police civilian personnel involved in 15 different operations.

Examples from around the world

◆ **Africa**
The UN has campaigned against apartheid; helped to prevent unrest in the Central African Republic; established peacekeeping forces in Sierra Leone, Ethiopia and Eritrea.

◆ **Asia**
Peacekeeping in Cambodia (1992-93); international security force sent to East Timor in 1999; offer to help restore democracy in Afghanistan after overthrow of Taliban.

◆ **Europe**
The former Yugoslavia – four UN missions helped to secure the peace following the Dayton Peace Agreement. In 1999, following NATO bombing and the withdrawal of Yugoslav forces, the UN sent an international team to Kosovo to stabilise the administration of the area.

◆ **Central America**
The UN has worked to establish and sustain peace and democracy in Nicaragua, El Salvador, Guatemala and Haiti.

◆ **The Middle East**
During its existence, the UN has seen five full-scale wars and several other outbreaks of fierce fighting between Arabs and Israelis. Security Council resolutions have been passed, peacekeeping troops have been sent to the Golan Heights and to Southern Lebanon but the fighting goes on.
Since the Gulf War in 1991, a UN observer mission has been keeping watch on the border between Kuwait and Iraq.

◆ **War in Iraq**
The 2003 war in Iraq clearly showed some of the UN's difficulties. Kofi Annan, the UN Secretary-General, and the UN Security Council were unable to stop the USA-UK led coalition from attacking Iraq and was forced to withdraw UN weapons inspectors from Iraq before their work was completed. In the face of action from a superpower like the USA, there was little the UN could do.

What does the UN do to protect human rights?

The UN's Universal Declaration of Human Rights sets the standard on human rights. Most countries have agreed to uphold its principles. Important areas covered include the rights of women, the rights of the child, the status of refugees and the prevention of genocide. The UN Commission on Human Rights reviews the performance of countries on human rights and can appoint international experts to report on human rights abuses.

The UN and international law

The UN has been able to secure agreement on the law of the sea and drug trafficking. It is also through the United Nations that the massive violations of international law which took place during conflict in the former Yugoslavia were investigated. To help to bring war criminals to justice, an International Criminal Court was established in 1998.

Humanitarian assistance

When disaster strikes, the UN can organise food, shelter and medicine for victims. During 1999, $1.4 billion was raised from member countries to help 26 million people. In 1997-98, the UN helped 51 countries to cope with 77 natural disasters. This has been at great human cost. Since 1992, almost 200 UN civilian staff have been killed and a similar number taken hostage.

The United Nations gave assistance after the tsunami catastrophe of 2004 where homes, schools, and local communities had been destroyed.

The Specialised Agencies

Much of the work of the United Nations is channelled through its specialised agencies, which employ experts to carry out work in their fields. Though they are closely connected to the UN, these agencies run their own affairs.

◆ **UNICEF (The United Nations Children's Fund)**
Works in 150 countries, running programmes on immunisation, primary health care, nutrition and basic education. UNICEF spends more than $800 million a year. War and civil unrest have separated 1 million children from their parents and made 12 million more homeless. In 1998, UNICEF joined with other UN agencies, including the World Health Organisation (WHO), to fight malaria. AIDS is being tackled in the same way. UNICEF established children's rights when, in 1990, the Convention on the Rights of the Child became international law.

◆ **WHO (World Health Organisation)**
80 million children have been immunised against six killer diseases. The WHO's efforts eradicated smallpox in 1980. The WHO has saved 7 million children from river blindness in Africa.

◆ FAO (Food and Agriculture Organisation)

The FAO has helped Asian rice farmers to improve crop yields, saving them $12 million on pesticides and saving governments $150 million on pesticide subsidies. The FAO has also supported plans for the sustainable development of tropical forests.

Does the UN work?

The United Nations clearly has a huge number of successes to its credit, but there are still some reservations about its performance:

- War and famine are still regular occurrences in developing countries. The Middle East, after fifty years of UN involvement, is no nearer to peace. There have been many 'smaller' wars. Nuclear weapons still exist in large numbers.
- Too many member countries choose to ignore the UN when it suits, e.g., 'sanctions-busting'.
- Because member states have control over their own affairs, the UN sometimes cannot intervene quickly enough.
- The UN has fought in a war in the Gulf. Is this really keeping the peace?
- The UN lacks 'teeth'. Children are still being exploited, both as child labourers and even as soldiers, within member countries which have signed the Convention on the Rights of the Child.
- Global warming has not been checked.
- The World Bank has a poor record on the debt of developing countries.
- The permanent members wield too much influence through the Security Council.
- The UN is not democratic.
- The UN is a club of governments. This can block rather than encourage change.

The European Union

The twenty-five members of the EU make up a very powerful economic force. The EU started in the 1950s with six member countries seeking to organise trade with one other to mutual advantage (the 'Common Market'). Over the years, the EU has extended both its membership and its aims. It is now very much concerned with social, legal and economic policies. More recently, there have been suggestions for an EU military force.

Why countries join the EU

- it provides markets for their goods;
- it allows their citizens access to jobs;
- it gives consumers a wider choice;
- they become part of a powerful economic grouping;
- problems and disagreements among nations can be discussed through the EU;
- it is a way of establishing human rights over an increasing number of countries.

How the EU works

The Parliament

The 25 member states directly elect 732 Members of the European Parliament (MEPs), including 78 from the UK, by proportional representation to the Parliament. There are elections every five years and the MEPs sit in political, rather than national, groupings. The European Parliament has power to:

- set the EU budget – its most important function and the area in which it can wield most power;
- pass laws;
- scrutinise the work of the Commission.

The Council of Ministers

This body consists of government representatives from each member country. The Council meets to consider the most important issues concerning the future direction of the EU. The Council of Ministers can change in composition from meeting to meeting. If the matter under discussion is of vital importance then the Prime Ministers of each country will attend. If, however, global warming is under discussion then environment ministers may attend. Again, the make-up of the Council will change if there is a general election in one of the member countries and a different party of government takes office.

Negotiations in the Council do not always lead to agreement and sometimes member countries are allowed to 'opt out' of parts of an agreement.

The Commission

Each member of the European Union nominates one member of the Commission. Each member of the Commission has a particular area of responsibility to look after, eg, transport.

The UK has always nominated former politicians. However, when they take up posts with the European Commission their political party and national loyalties have to be put aside and they have to work in the interests of the European Union as a whole. The members of the Commission are the civil servants of the EU, making sure that EU policies are properly put into effect. They are also required to bring forward suggestions for new laws for the EU. The Commission cannot pass laws – only the Parliament can do that.

In October 2004, the new President of the European Commission was forced to withdraw his proposals for new commissioners. This was the result of opposition from MEPs to one commissioner who had expressed personal opinions many MEPs disagreed with. MEPs showed that they were not willing simply to 'rubber-stamp' the new commissioners without making their views known. Many people feel that clashes between elected MEPs and unelected commissioners will become more frequent as the European Parliament tries to assert its authority in the future.

The Court of Justice

This Court decides whether European law has been correctly applied. There are occasions where national laws and European laws come into conflict.

The 'Bosman ruling' in football was an example of European law being placed above national law. However, the European Court does not work quickly and cases sometimes take years to be dealt with.

Other important EU bodies

◆ the European Regional Development Fund;
◆ the Agriculture Guidance and Guarantee Fund;
◆ the Social Fund.

Current issues for the EU

◆ **Expansion**
The EU intends to expand its membership further from the present 25 countries. The EU feels that it is important to welcome as many nations as possible into the EU.

Many of the former Communist countries of Eastern Europe do not have a strong tradition of democracy, do not have advanced economies and have not always enjoyed a wide range of human rights. Bringing them into the EU would help to develop all these areas and to make sure that conflict between European countries would be less likely. Countries wishing to join have to meet standards of democracy, social welfare (including human rights) and economic development. Some applicants are finding these standards hard to meet.

Bulgaria and Romania may well be next to join, while Croatia, Turkey and Macedonia are also in the queue.

As the EU grows, there will be changes to the structure of Parliament and the Commission, resulting in a drop in numbers from existing larger

member countries. This may reduce their power and influence on the operation and direction of the EU. There will also be economic issues arising from expansion. The average GDP per head of the ten new members is 40% of the average of the 'old' members. Some long-standing members fear that they will 'lose out' as European Union resources are aimed at the less well-off members.

◆ **The Euro**
This is the currency, or money, which the EU hopes all members will trade in. Twelve member countries (but not Britain) agreed to replace their national currencies with the Euro in 2002.

◆ **Rapid Reaction Force**
Many members of the EU are also members of military alliances such as NATO. Some have recently been involved in the use of force in the former Yugoslavia. The EU, however, has never had a military force of its own.
Recently, members have agreed to set up such a military force. Some people are concerned that this force may undermine NATO. Others question where it might be used.

◆ **Agriculture**
The continuing high cost of the Common Agricultural Policy (CAP) and the threat of BSE are matters of great concern to EU members.

◆ **Constitution**
In October 2004, the member countries of the European Union agreed on a new constitution. However, there is opposition to the new constitution within member countries, not all of whom may eventually accept the new constitution.

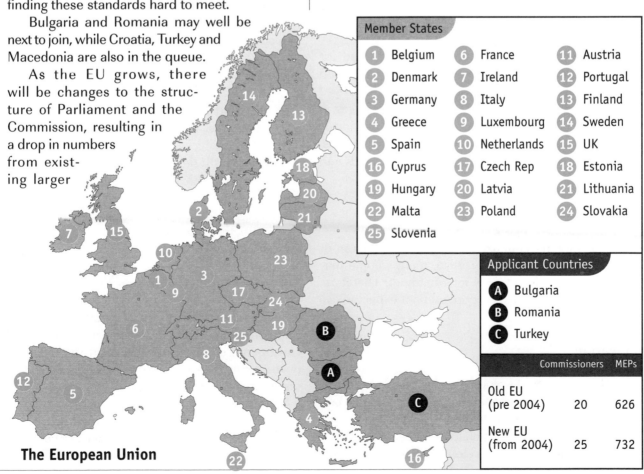

The European Union

Member States

1	Belgium	6	France	11	Austria
2	Denmark	7	Ireland	12	Portugal
3	Germany	8	Italy	13	Finland
4	Greece	9	Luxembourg	14	Sweden
5	Spain	10	Netherlands	15	UK
16	Cyprus	17	Czech Rep	18	Estonia
19	Hungary	20	Latvia	21	Lithuania
22	Malta	23	Poland	24	Slovakia
25	Slovenia				

Applicant Countries

A Bulgaria
B Romania
C Turkey

	Commissioners	MEPs
Old EU (pre 2004)	20	626
New EU (from 2004)	25	732

Politics of Aid – Identifying Needs

Population growth

Population growth in many developing countries is very rapid. This means that more food, schools, hospitals and homes have to be provided. Overpopulation is caused by mothers giving birth to many babies because it is traditional to do so. In addition, some do not use contraception because of lack of availability or for moral or religious reasons.

Not enough food

In many developing countries, there are too many people for the available supplies of food. Sometimes, insufficient food is grown because of drought or poor quality land. In other cases, land is used for cash crops for export. This earns some cash for farmers but feeds people outside the country rather than those who live locally. This method of farming may be unsuitable in the longer term. Some countries encourage their farmers to plant cash crops. This is fine if the world price for the crop remains high and the crop does not fail. However, if the farmers do not get a good crop, they fall into debt, lose their land and cannot feed their families.

Even when enough food is grown, it may be poorly distributed.

Poor land

Much of Africa's land surface cannot be used for farming. Mountains and deserts cannot be cultivated to support life. Also, food supplies can be destroyed by disease, by pests like the locust or by changes in the climate. Climate changes can destroy previously productive areas. Floods can wash away soil, crops, animals and homes. Droughts can turn grasslands into deserts.

Health

Many developing countries have too few doctors or hospitals for the population. Also, many people may not be able to afford to pay for treatment. Therefore, the death rate is high and people do not expect to live to a very old age.

Education

Schooling in many developing countries is very basic. Boys may learn the basics of reading and counting but, frequently, girls remain illiterate. Their place is looking after the home and bearing children. These factors have had a bad effect on the development of the economy and the provision of social welfare in the country. When a machine breaks down, few can read the repair manuals so it rusts away and remains out of use. People who cannot read cannot become engineers, doctors, nurses or teachers.

Low standard of living

Most developing countries depend either on mining, forestry or agriculture for their economies or on providing cheap labour to manufacture or assemble goods for companies to sell to the developed world. This means that the companies make big profits while the people of the country work for very, very low wages and have very low living standards.

War

Often trade is not carried out for the benefit of the people. Many poor countries spend a great deal on military equipment to threaten their neighbours or to keep their citizens in order.

Wars can destroy farms, towns or factories. In addition, this can lead to refugees, epidemics, starvation and death. Most of all, it destroys a country's resources and prevents it from becoming better off.

Debt

Developing countries have borrowed large amounts of money to build up their own industries, confident that the loans would be repaid. When this doesn't happen, the developing countries are so deep in debt that they find it hard even to pay back the interest. This debt crisis means that more money flows from poor countries to rich countries than is returned in the form of aid.

Needs of developing countries

The main need of every developing country is to improve living standards. This may require the country to:

- reduce birth rates;
- improve health provision;
- improve education standards;
- improve agriculture;
- restructure the economy;
- redirect resources.

Aid to developing countries

Many developing countries are working hard to solve their problems. The needs of developing countries can be met by better planning and more careful use of resources. However, more powerful countries and organisations can help by providing aid. Without aid, most developing countries would not be able to develop their social and economic infrastructures.

Governments of better-off countries have tried to help, mostly for humanitarian reasons. In addition, some of the worst affected countries have close historical ties with European countries which had 'discovered' and colonised them in previous centuries.

Some commentators have argued that when pictures of the Ethiopian famine of the early nineteen-eighties were televised then citizens of developed countries realised the scale of the problem.

Why do some countries need aid?

◆ Some countries have a position and climate which leaves them open to natural disasters – Bangladesh (floods), El Salvador (earthquake). Frequently, homes and farms are destroyed.

◆ Climate can affect food supplies. By 2002, Ethiopia was in the fourth year of a drought. Harvests have been disastrous. There is, in developing countries, a death from hunger every 4 seconds.

◆ Countries suffering from natural disasters often do not have the resources to prevent 'knock-on' effects, e.g., contamination of water supply leading to epidemics of cholera, dysentery and death.

◆ Civil war, perhaps involving genocide (Rwanda), often leads to food shortages, destruction of homes and to hospital and medical facilities being over-whelmed. Situations are made worse if government breaks down.

◆ 'New' illnesses such as Aids can cause havoc. Affected countries are too poor to afford the drugs needed.

◆ Developing countries are struggling to establish modern economies. They do not have the money, knowledge or technology to respond to sudden demands.

◆ Problems in one country can cause refugees to flee into a neighbouring country, making the situation even more difficult to deal with.

Forms of aid

The countries of the developed world give money in three main ways:

◆ Bilateral aid – given by one country to another. Most of the aid given in this way benefits the donor country. The country giving aid can set a number of conditions which the recipient country must agree to in order to get the aid. For this reason, most of bilateral aid is tied aid. Although this type of aid may help a country to meet some of its needs, it puts the donor countries in a powerful position.

◆ Multilateral aid – given by many countries through one organisation such as the United Nations, the European Union or the World Bank. The countries can decide how the aid is to be spent to satisfy need. Normally, it will not have to be repaid.

◆ Voluntary aid is usually raised by charities such as OXFAM and Save the Children through donations and sponsorship.

Who provides aid?

Aid is collected and directed through many agencies:

◆ the United Nations and its Specialised Agencies;
◆ other international organisations such as the EU;
◆ individual countries – the UK has an International Development department;
◆ independent international organisations – the Red Cross/Red Crescent;
◆ charitable organisations of long standing - Oxfam;
◆ church-based organisations – SCIAF;
◆ Voluntary Service Overseas (VSO).

The general public has become more involved in aid in recent years, supporting 'Band Aid 20' and 'Red Nose Days'. Aid can also take many other forms – 'adopting' a school, buying produce from developing countries at fair prices and so on. Examples of some of the ways in which aid can be offered and delivered.

◆ Money – either by grants or loans. Many people in the developed world are uneasy about the level of debt which developing countries are now facing. Some aid is 'tied', i.e., the loan has to be spent in the donor country, on specified goods. This may mean that the goods purchased are not always the best choices to meet the needs of the buying na-tions. There is also a suspicion that the rulers of less democratic countries do not always use the aid in areas of most need.
Democracy is taking hold in the developing world and there is a growing demand, led by groups such as Jubilee 2000, and recently met in part by the UK, to wipe out the debt. This will give developing coun-tries the chance to make economic progress.

◆ Advice on how to grow crops more productively. The United Nations – through its Specialised Agency, the FAO – has been helping developing countries for many decades.

◆ Food - emergency supplies of food have been sent to meet crises, especially in Africa. In the long run, however, it is better if countries can produce enough food supplies of their own.

◆ Expert help – British rescue teams went to the earthquake zone in India in January 2001 to use the most up-to-date equipment to search for survivors. Medical staff can also be sent to crisis areas.

◆ Goods – charitable organisations can organise the collection of books and clothing to send to devel-oping countries. Businesses can offer machinery which may be out of date in an advanced country but very useful to a developing country.

ⓘ Remember

There is no point in sending computers if what is needed is picks and shovels!

How to Study for Standard Grade Modern Studies

There is no point in sending computers if what is needed is picks and shovels!

People learn in different ways. However, there are a number of common factors which will help most people.

Where to work

Try to ensure you have a place which is:

- quiet so that people will not disturb you;
- comfortable for you to work in. This might mean a large desk and chair;
- uncluttered but with all the equipment needed close at hand;
- free from distractions;
- well lit.

Managing your time

If you are studying for seven or eight Standard Grade exams, you may feel that you don't have enough time to study. However, if you start to revise early and manage your time carefully, this should not be a problem.

    Work through the following calculation and put in your own results, as it may help you realise how much time is available.

1.	How many hours are there in a week?	7 x 24 =	168 hours
2.	How much time do you spend in class?	30x50/55 minutes =	27.5 hours
3.	How long do you sleep for?	9 x 7 =	63 hours
4.	How long do you work for?		10 hours
5.	How much free time do you want each day?	2 x 7 =	14

Total hours use = 14 + 10 + 63 + 27.5 = 114.5 hours = 168 - 114.5 = 53.5 hours

This means that you have 53.5 hours each week in which you could study. This would give you eight hours every day. Nobody would expect to study for this time. However, if you could do an extra two hours every day, what a difference it might make. This would still allow you to do the other things that you like doing. It would also help if you were to plan out your study times on a timetable. Your studying could be organised in such a way that you can still do all your other activities/hobbies.

Time	Monday	Tuesday	Wednesday	Thursday	Friday	Saturday	Sunday
8 – 10							
10 – 12							
12 – 2							
2 – 4							
4 – 6							
6 – 8							
8 – 10							
10 – 12							

It is not a good idea to work for too long. It is better to work in short bursts. This will help you to apply yourself 100% to your studies.

Time management in the exam

The Credit paper lasts two hours. In the paper you will find 4 questions, each made up of 2, 3 or 4 parts. You should spend 30 minutes on each full question. Try to think about how you will use your time before you go into the exam.

The General paper lasts 1 hour and 30 minutes. In the paper you will find 4 questions. Each question is usually worth 16 marks (two four mark questions on Knowledge and Understanding and two four mark questions on Enquiry Skills). You should spend about 22 minutes on each of these questions. Questions on Investigating may be worth between 2 and 4 marks.

Preparing for the exam

In the Standard Grade Modern Studies exam you will have to complete Knowledge and Understanding and Enquiry Skills questions. You may need to use different methods to prepare for the different parts.

Knowledge and Understanding (KU)

Knowledge and Understanding questions will test your understanding of the information in the course. You will need to be able to recall a number of points. This section will highlight some of the methods which could be used to help you to retain all the facts. These include note taking; mind maps; spider diagrams; acronyms; daft sentences. However, this does not mean that there aren't other effective methods of learning information.

Note Taking

In the Standard Grade course you will have studied a number of different topics over a two year period. If you were to try and remember all this information from your jotter, it would be a very difficult task. However, the following hints might help to make it more manageable.

First, you need to work out what you need to know. On pages 5, 16, 30 and 48 you will find a list of exam questions. It would help you to organise your notes if you put a number of key ideas or points under each of the exam questions. When you have finished this for each section, ask someone to check that all your examples are relevant and that you have not missed any out.

Remember to check through your jotter, notebook, folder, class notes and text books. If you have 5 or 6 pieces of relevant information, then you should have enough material to use in the exam.

> ### ⓘ Important
>
> **N.B. You must be able to explain each of these pieces of relevant information.**

Some people like to make notes using spider diagrams. This helps to lay out the information more clearly.

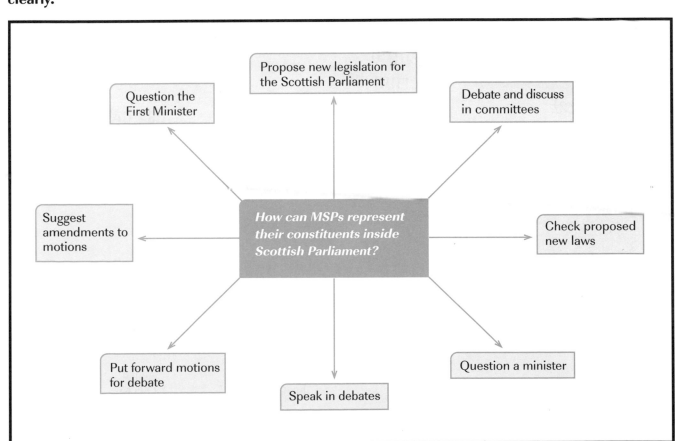

Other students like to use Mind Maps. They are very much like Spider Diagrams only they also include colour and pictures. For some people this makes it much easier to learn.

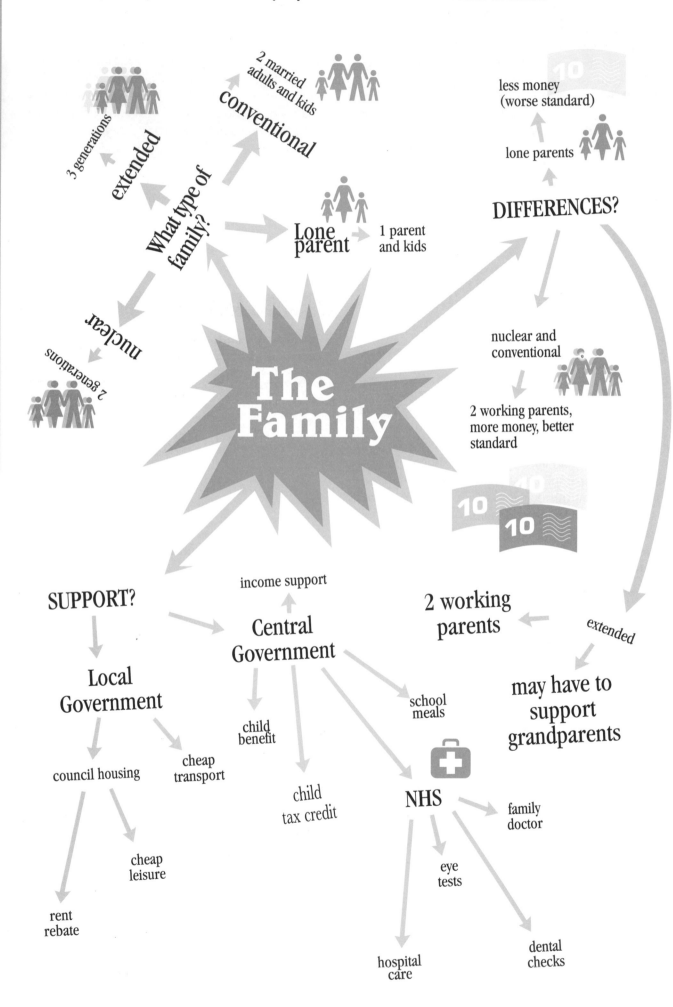

Other methods used to learn facts include:

◆ Acronyms – where each letter stands for a point or word. If you were trying to think of advantages of joining NATO, you could use "busmen"!

b	–	back }
u	–	up } in war
s	–	strong defence
m	–	more power
e	–	end world wars
n	–	new status if you join

◆ making up silly sentences. If you are trying to re-member a number of points, it may help if you try to make up a silly sentence using the first letter from each of the points. Sometimes, the sillier the sentence is, the more likely you are to remember the points. Thus if you were trying to give the ar-guments for the electoral system used to elect the Scottish Parliament, you could use:

"Few voters can get stupid lines."

This would mean:
- *Few Votes are wasted.*
- *Coalition Government.*
- *Strong Links (with MSPs).*

◆ recording information and then playing it back;
◆ trying to remember relevant facts and asking people to question you;
◆ going for long walks and trying to think important issues through;
◆ recording points on large pieces of paper and sticking them to the wall (obviously with parent's permission);
◆ typing notes into a computer.

Questions under examination conditions

When you think you have learned the facts from one area of the course, you should try to complete a past paper question under exam conditions. This will show you whether or not there are any gaps in your knowl-edge. Ask your teacher to check your work. He or she may also be able to give you pointers.

Enquiry Skills (ES)

There are five types of Enquiry Skills questions:
1. detecting examples of exaggeration, bias and se-lective use of facts;
2. making comparisons and drawing conclusions;
3. expressing support for a point of view;
4. giving aims for an investigation and explaining what methods of enquiry should be used;
5. showing awareness of the advantages and disad-vantages of different methods of enquiry.

Types 1 to 3 require students to use sources. Types 4 and 5 require students to plan out investigations and think of the advantages and disadvantages of methods of enquiry. The best way to study for these questions is to complete questions under exam conditions and ask someone to check your answers (see section on how to answer exam questions).

How to Answer Examination Questions

Standard Grade Modern Studies questions may cover:

◆ Knowledge and Understanding;
◆ Enquiry Skills based on sources given;
◆ Enquiry Skills based on investigating.

Knowledge and Understanding (KU)

Knowledge and Understanding (KU) questions will test what you know about the Standard Grade course and your understanding of the concepts that form the main framework of the course (see p68 for a more detailed explanation of what the concepts mean).

When answering Knowledge and Understanding questions you should:

◆ check how many marks the question is worth. For every two marks you should explain a point fully and relate it to the question. Thus if the question is worth 8 marks, you will need to include 4 developed points.
◆ make sure that every point relates to the question being asked. After every point check that you are still answering the question set.

If you were asked:

"Explain, in detail, the main arguments for expanding the membership of the European Union." (KU, 8 marks)

You should give 4 arguments for expanding the membership. However, if you started to give the arguments against, you would get no marks for those points relating to arguments against.

◆ Relate every point to the question asked.
◆ Do not make lists, if you do you will be given a **maximum** of half marks. It is much better to select a few points and explain them in detail.

Thus, if you were asked:

"What methods can pressure groups use to influence MSPs?" (KU, 4 marks)

You could state that:

Pressure groups can use lots of methods to influence

MSPs including marches, demonstrations, lobbying, letters to newspapers and MSPs, petitions, blockades, providing MSPs with information, providing sponsorship to the MSP and holding meetings.

This is a list and would be given half marks. It would be much better to pick two and explain them in detail.

◆ Make sure that you answer all aspects of a question.

Thus, if you were asked:

"Describe, in detail, the political rights and responsibilities of UK citizens." (KU, 6 marks)

You would have to explain points about the rights and responsibilities to get all 6 marks. Below, you will find two answers given full marks for a Standard Grade KU question.

"Describe the social and economic factors which have made it difficult for women to participate effectively in trade unions in recent years." (KU, 6 marks)

*One social problem is prejudice. Some trade unionists think that women are not equal with men and will not allow them to **participate** effectively. This means that they will vote for male **representatives**, even when they are not as qualified as the women. Another social problem is discrimination. Women are not given equal rights to take a full part in the decision making of the union. Their views are sometimes ignored or made fun of.*

An economic factor is that women often work on a part-time basis. This means that they cannot afford to pay the union subscription and therefore take no part in union activity. Another economic factor is that women work in industries which refuse to allow trade unions. This means that they don't get the opportunity to join.

> ⌛ **Note**
>
> **There are at least 3 points which have been explained, the candidate has used the concepts of the course (participation and representation) and economic and social arguments are discussed.**

"Give two reasons why immigrants might wish to live in the USA." (KU, 4)

Immigrants might wish to live in the USA because they believe in the 'American Dream'. That is, they think that in America everyone is free and, if you work hard enough, you can become very rich. They might also think that it is a much better place because there is no real poverty, wars or political persecution in America. This will mean that their children will have the opportunity to live a good life, with the benefits of a high standard of living, good education and many job vacancies.

> ### ⓘ Note
> - **Two points have been given.**
> - **They are not listed.**
> - **They are explained and relate to the question.**

Source-based Enquiry Skills questions

All source-based Enquiry Skills questions ask candidates to make direct use of sources which are provided. These questions can be divided into 3 main types – those that ask candidates to:

- identify and explain a lack of objectivity (e.g., exaggeration, bias and selective use of facts);
- compare sources and draw conclusions;
- give arguments for and against a personal or given point of view.

Enquiry Skills questions – to find and explain a lack of objectivity

"All Americans enjoy high standards of living."
American Journalist

Using the table below, give two reasons why the journalist could be accused of exaggeration. (ES, 4 marks)

This question is worth 4 marks. Therefore, a good answer must:

- include 2 points taken from the source with explanation;
- explain how the journalist has exaggerated.

How to answer this type of question

Plan your answer.

- **Step 1:**
  Find out what the question is asking you to do. You need to find the pieces of evidence which will show that the journalist has exaggerated
- **Step 2:**
  Identify what the journalist is saying.
  "All Americans enjoy high standards of living."
- **Step 3:**
  Spot the exaggeration and explain it. In 2004, only 8.2% of Whites lived below the poverty level compared to 22.5% of Hispanic families. In 2004, unemployment for Hispanics was 6.7% but only 4.7% for Whites. Both points show that **all** Americans don't enjoy a high standard of living.

An answer worth 4 marks might look like this:

The journalist might be accused of exaggeration when he says that "all Americans enjoy high standards of living". He is exaggerating because many families live below the poverty line, and 8.2% of Whites and 22.5% of Hispanic families have a low standard of living.

Also in 2004, unemployment for Hispanics was 6.7% but for Whites it was only 4.7%. To have a high standard of living you need a job. Thus many Hispanics and Whites will not have a high standard of living.

> ### Notes
> - **2 points are given;**
> - **2 pieces of evidence from the source are used;**
> - **each point of exaggerated is explained.**

USA 2004 unemployment rates, families living below the poverty level and households with incomes greater than $50,000 for both White Americans and Hispanic Americans		
	White Americans	Hispanic Americans
Unemployment	4.7%	6.7%
Families living below the poverty level	8.2%	22.5%

Enquiry Skills question – to compare sources and draw conclusions

Study sources 1 and 2 below, then answer the question which follows:

Source 1

"There are over 659 MPs in the House of Commons, yet less than 20% of them are women. This is a ridiculous situation.
    Women make up over half the population. Half the candidates for each party should be women. This is the only way to deal with this discrimination."

Source 2

"The number of female MPs in the House of Commons has increased greatly. In 1983, there were only 23. By 2001 there were 118.
    MPs should be chosen on ability and not because they are male or female. To insist on half the candidates being women is a form of discrimination."

Sources 1 and 2 give different views about the representation of women in the House of Commons.

Using your own words, say what the differences are. Mention two differences in your answer. (Enquiry Skills, 4 marks)

How to answer this type of question

◆   **Step 1: Find out what the question is looking for.**
For example, in what ways do the views about women in the House of Commons differ.

◆   **Step 2: Find ways in which the two sources are different.**
For example, in source 1 it states that less than 20% of the 659 MPs are women while in source 2 it states that the number of women MPs has increased from 23 in 1983 to 118 in 2001.
In source 1 it states that half the candidates for each party should be women but in source 2 it states that it would be discrimination to make 50% of candidates female.

◆   **Step 3: Write your answer.**
The sources have very different views about the representation of women in the House of Commons. In source 1 it states that they have not

made much progress because less than 20% of the MPs are women. However, source 2 states that they have made progress because the number of women MPs has increased from 23 in 1983 to 118 in 2001.
They also disagree on how to improve matters. Source 1 states that half the candidates for each party should be women but source 2 thinks that this would be unfair.

> ### ⚙ Note
>
> Both sources have been used and a direct comparison has been made between the two sources.

Enquiry Skills question – to give arguments for and against a given or personal point of view

Study sources 1 and 2 below, then answer the question which follows.

Source 1

Unemployment
Claimant Count (2000-2004)

Source 2

Unemployment levels for Scottish regions and UK for 2004

Lothians	3.1
Highlands and Islands	5.2
Glasgow	7.7
Central Scotland	5.7
West of Scotland	4.7
South of Scotland	5.0
North East Scotland	3.1
Mid Scotland and Fife	4.6
UK	**3.2**

Extract from a government report

"In recent years, the unemployment rate throughout Scotland has been higher than the United Kingdom average."

Using sources **1** and **2** above, provide evidence **for** and **against** the view stated in the government report.

(Enquiry Skills, 4 marks)

How to answer this type of question

> ### Note
>
> ◆ **Use both sources for full marks.**
> ◆ **Half marks for only one source.**
> ◆ **Provide for and against for full marks. Half marks for only for or against.**

Plan your answer

◆ **Step 1:** Identify what the statement is saying. For example, in recent years the unemployment rate in Scotland has been higher than the UK average.

◆ **Step 2:** Identify evidence supporting this view from Source 1 and Source 2.

◆ **Step 3:** Identify arguments against this view using source 1 and 2.

Possible Answer

In recent years, Scotland has had a poorer employment record than the UK. Source 1 shows that throughout the period 2000 to 2004 the unemployment rate in Scotland remained higher than the UK average.

While it is true that unemployment in Scotland fell from approximately 4.2% to approximately 2.7% during the period 2000 to 2004, the UK average also fell from approximately 4.0% to just over 2.6% during the same period.

To some extent source 2 supports this conclusion as in 2004 Highlands and Islands, Glasgow, Central Scotland, West of Scotland, South of Scotland and Mid Scotland and Fife all had unemployment rates above the UK average.

Opposing this view however, is evidence from source 2 which shows that certain parts of Scotland enjoyed an unemployment rate below the UK average in 2004. For example, both Lothians and North East Scotland recorded an unemployment rate of 3.1% and this is slightly lower than the recorded UK average unemployment rate of 3.2% for 2004.

The evidence shows that although it is generally true to state that the unemployment rate in Scotland

has been higher than the UK average some parts of Scotland did manage to record an unemployment rate that was lower than the UK average.

This was a good answer because it:

◆ used both sources;
◆ gave arguments for and against;
◆ used information from sources well to analyse all aspects of question;
◆ related the points to the question.

Enquiry Skills question – to produce a hypothesis and headings to help investigate an issue and describe and justify methods that could be used to find the information.

Possible question

You have been asked to carry out an investigation on the topic below:

Investigation topic – the groups which try to help the elderly to meet their needs.

(a) State a relevant hypothesis for your investigation. (Enquiry Skills, 2 marks)

(b) Give two aims or headings to help you to prove or disprove your hypothesis. (Enquiry Skills, 2 marks)

(c) You decide to use the internet to help you with your investigation. For one of your chosen aims or headings, describe how you would find information using the internet. (Enquiry Skills, 2 marks)

(d) You also decide to use a questionnaire. Describe, in detail, two possible advantages of a questionnaire as a method of collecting information for this investigation. (Enquiry Skills, 4 marks)

Some hints

◆ To answer question (a) you must first understand what is meant by a hypothesis. At the most basic level, a hypothesis is a statement that you want to test to see if it is true or false.

Thus the hypothesis:

"The Government meets the needs of all elderly people in the UK."

could be tested. However, the following statements are not hypotheses because they cannot be tested:

"Groups which try to help the elderly."
"Local Government and the elderly."

◆ To answer question (b) you have to produce aims or headings which will help you to test your hypothesis. For example:

Hypothesis

"The government meets the needs of all elderly people in the UK."

Aim

- What does the government do to meet the needs of the elderly?
- How effectively does the government meet the needs of the elderly?
- Do other groups help to meet the needs of the elderly?

When you have completed your aims, check to make sure they will help to prove or disprove your hypothesis.

◆ To answer part (c) you must describe how the internet could be used to find information which could be used to test your hypothesis.

You must try to explain in detail how the internet could be used. For example, you could write:

The internet could be used to find information by using a search engine to find a relevant web-site. This will help me to see if the government meets the needs of all the elderly. It might allow me to look at government sites, sites of pressure groups which work for the elderly, local government sites and private businesses.

ⓘ Note

The point has been explained in some detail.

◆ Possible answer to question (d) from the previous section.

Researchers will use a questionnaire to find information because they know that, from a sample of people, they will be able to predict the results from the whole population. This will make it quick and easy to find out what people think about an issue. They will also use a questionnaire because they know that they will get a good response because they will go and ask the people individually. This will help to ensure that the results are useful and conclusions can be drawn from the sample about the whole population.

Enquiry Skills question – show understanding of the advantages and disadvantages of methods used to collect information for an investigation.

This question demands that you understand both the advantages and disadvantages of methods which may be used by social scientists to collect information about a topic they may be studying. The methods you need to know about are as follows.

Interrogation of databases or files

Advantages
- ✓ a large amount of information in the form of a table;
- ✓ the information is brief and to the point;
- ✓ you need only take out the information you need;
- ✓ information can be viewed on-screen or printed out.

Disadvantages
- ✗ results must be interpreted;
- ✗ databases often contain only facts and figures – no analysis;
- ✗ you almost always need a PC to access databases – not convenient;
- ✗ interrogation can be time-consuming.

Internet

Advantages
- ✓ holds information from many valuable sources;
- ✓ now widely available;
- ✓ sites regularly updated;
- ✓ holds data in many forms – written, graphic, photo, video;
- ✓ quick to access;
- ✓ you can take print-outs.

Disadvantages
- ✗ you need a PC with modem;
- ✗ costs money to use;
- ✗ can offer too much information – it is time-consuming.

Questionnaire

Advantages
- ✓ important questions asked;
- ✓ relatively cheap;
- ✓ easy to get people to answer;
- ✓ questions can be geared to your exact needs;
- ✓ responses easily pulled together;
- ✓ gives time to analyse results.

Disadvantages
- ✗ questions must be made up with care;
- ✗ needs a high number of responses to be valid;
- ✗ responses must usually be collected within a short time-scale;
- ✗ questions usually have to be 'yes' or 'no' for consistency;
- ✗ need to ensure that an appropriate sample (group of respondents) is chosen.

Attitude survey

Advantages

- ✓ allows measurement of factors which cannot be put into figures;
- ✓ gives people the chance to express opinions;
- ✓ good for 'conscience' issues such as capital punishment, abortion.

Disadvantages

- ✗ needs extreme care when making up;
- ✗ more difficult to analyse responses;
- ✗ need to ensure that respondents are chosen carefully.

Structured interview

Advantages

- ✓ allows one-to-one interview with people who have the information you need;
- ✓ allows 'in-depth' questions;
- ✓ interesting answers can be followed up there and then;
- ✓ interview can be extended/cut short depending on progress;
- ✓ gives chance to explore an interviewee's opinions.

Disadvantages

- ✗ interviewee may not respond well to questions;
- ✗ you may misinterpret what was said;
- ✗ answers may be very personal – less useful for research.

Structured letter

Advantages

- ✓ simple and cheap to make up and send;
- ✓ good for simple answers to straightforward questions;
- ✓ relatively quick;
- ✓ personal communication – often more likely to get an answer.

Disadvantages

- ✗ questions need to be kept simple – limits value of letter;
- ✗ not everyone replies – some groups receive too many letters from Modern Studies pupils!
- ✗ You may just get a standard reply or a pile of publicity material which doesn't really answer your questions.

Structured observation/field work

Advantages

- ✓ allows you to observe 'real' behaviour;
- ✓ you can choose a time and place for observation.

Disadvantages

- ✗ people may alter their behaviour because you are there;
- ✗ may be very difficult to interpret your results;
- ✗ people may resent being observed;
- ✗ requires a very high degree of skill to observe well.

Library research

Advantages

- ✓ huge amount of material available;
- ✓ material organised under familiar catalogue system;
- ✓ photocopies can be made of relevant sources;
- ✓ books usually indexed – speeds up research;
- ✓ access usually free;
- ✓ professional help on hand;
- ✓ atmosphere helps study!
- ✓ Libraries have other sources of information - microfiche, recordings, video, internet.

Disadvantages

- ✗ there can be too much material;
- ✗ care needed to establish accuracy of sources;
- ✗ you may not get the books you need;
- ✗ library not always open.

Interrogation of TV/video/newspaper

Advantages

- ✓ cheap and accessible;
- ✓ TV up-to-date;
- ✓ can usually be re-read/replayed;
- ✓ newspapers often have analysis of issues;
- ✓ TV will usually have different political balance – more than one side of story.

Disadvantages

- ✗ most newspapers politically biased;
- ✗ TV news items often very short – little analysis;
- ✗ Some TV programmes discredited in the past for being misleading;
- ✗ Not always reliable – 'don't let the facts get in the way of a good story'.

Try to make sure that you can explain 2 arguments for and against each method.

Concepts and the Modern Studies Course

The concepts of the course will be tested in Knowledge and Understanding questions. They may be applied to a number of different examples in different parts of the exam. It is therefore important that you understand them and it will improve your mark if you can use them correctly to answer the questions set.

The concepts which you need to understand are:

Participation
This looks at the different ways in which people take part or don't take part in politics, trade unions and pressure groups. You may also be asked about different types of participation in the USA, Russia and China.

Representation
The ways in which different representatives are elected and how they look after the interests of the individuals who elected them. Questions may be asked about representation on different levels, including MPs, MSPs, councillors and in the work place.

Rights and Responsibilities
In most societies, citizens have rights and responsibilities. However, they do tend to vary. You should have a knowledge of these rights and responsibilities in the UK and either the USA, Russia or China.

Equality
Differences exist within and between societies. It is important that you know why these differences exist and how they are measured. You could be asked about inequalities in the UK (including the elderly, the employed and the unemployed and families) and in either the USA, Russia or China.

Ideology
These are different views about the best way to provide for the needs of all the people. You should have a knowledge about these differences in the UK. You should also be aware of different views on the value of human rights, equality and dissent in either the USA, Russia or China.

Need
All humans have needs to satisfy. You should be aware of these needs, differences in the ways they are satisfied, how they change, how they are met by the government, the community and individuals and the extent to which views vary about this. It is important to understand how these points relate to the UK. You could also be asked about need in the developing world (Africa) and ways in which the UN, EU and NATO help to meet countries' needs.

Power
Relates to ways in which different countries try to meet their own interests and sometimes have to compete against others. You may need to look at military force, diplomatic persuasion, aid, sanctions and the law.